Now What

Endorsements/Praise for
Now What...

"Imagine your future self wrote a book about what you are going to do to become even more successful than you ever imagined possible. *Now What* is that book. Every page, every paragraph, every sentence is profound, practical, and immediately applicable. Ahmard is that rare author who speaks from his own experience, sharing personal discoveries of simple yet powerful steps he has taken to transform the quality of his life. It is easy to guarantee this book will do the same for you!"

—**Rob Pennington**, Ph.D., psychologist, and award-winning author

"Ahmard Vital shares five simple, yet profound steps to growth in your life. We have all encountered struggles in our lives. Ahmard has a unique way of teaching the strategy in overcoming those struggles by making clear sense of them in order for you to move to your next level. So, I ask you... now, what is next for you?"

—**Erik "Mr. Awesome" Swanson**, Thirteen Times #1 Bestseller, Speaker & Author of *The 13 Steps to Riches*

"My transition from professional sports to entrepreneurship has been a great experience because of leaders like Ahmard Vital. He sees the value bettering our communities by creating more leaders within our youth. His book "Now What" provides an amazing blueprint on how to overcome a transition of any kind."

—**Russell Shepard**, Seven-year NFL veteran and former high school All-American and Owner of Shep Boys Waste Management LLC

"*Now What* is a game changer! It's a primer for high performance results, both personally and professionally. If you're looking to up-level your life, this book is for you. It's a mustread—inspiring, informative, and instructional. Vital reveals proven principles and actionable strategies for success and achievement. If you're wondering, Now What?, wonder no longer. Get this book and find your answers. Vital lays them out. Excellent work."

—**Arthur J. Johnson,** Author, Lecturer and Peak Performance Thought Leader

"*Now What?* is a great read with thought-provoking insights! It contains many Biblical lessons that would have helped me when I was a younger, new Christian. As a parent and grandparent, I would highly recommend this book to the next generations as they chart their course and follow God's plan for their life."

—**Arni Jacobson,** Pastor and Author of *The Favor Factor* and *5 Keys to Reaching Your Family for Christ*

"There comes a time in each of our lives that a pivotal moment occurs, a moment where we say enough is enough, and we drive forward with passion and zeal. *Now What* is a wonderful journey through one man's life as he picks up the pieces of his past trauma and decides to move forward with his life. Childhood trauma stays with us and is associated with numerous adverse health outcomes unless we turn into the pain, face it, and ask ourselves what we will do going forward? Are we going to stay in the same place? Has this place helped me, my family, loved ones, or those in my social circle? Or am I going to reflect, decide, plan, act, seek, and finally have closure? Ahmard Vital has written a masterpiece outlining the human experience, a masterclass on resilience. The answer to Now What is given with a resounding, joyous leap forward."

—**Dr. Richard Harris,** Physician, Pharmacist, Entrepreneur with Great Health and Wellness

"Changing patterns in your life can be challenging, but incredibly rewarding. *Now What* lays out the repetitive path to create positive change in your life."

—**Dave Austin,** founder of Extreme Focus, author of *The Unfinished Cross* and *Be a Beast*

"*Now What* is a must read for anyone who's stuck and doesn't know where to begin. Packed with strategies and applicable knowledge, this is the survivors guide to beginning greatness."

—**Kevin Parker**, International Speaker, Coach, and Best-Selling Author of *Winning Against All Odds*

"If you're looking for simple solutions to improve your professional and personal life, *Now What* is exactly what you're looking for! Ahmard Vital lays out simple and practical steps that have proven results that will help you grow in every area of your life. This book has the answers you're seeking."

—**Shannon Parsons**, Speaker and Author

"*Now What* is a beautifully written and relatable book that hits the bullseye in terms of perspective. Many times in my own complicated life when I feel wronged I have asked myself the question of 'why?' I should have been asking myself the question, "now what?" In an increasingly complicated world, *Now What* serves as a blueprint for success that should be read by every young adult seeking inspiration in their daily lives to get up and go get whatever it is they desire."

—**Brandon Batch**, Chairman of the Board, Rope Youth Midland (Texas)

"Working with today's youth is very special because you have to connect with them. It helps to know their history and understand their environment to keep them inspired. *Now What* is a needed resource that can assist young people within the community to become successful. Ahmard Vital is an individual who knows the culture and has the ability to reach those who need it most. I highly recommend this book."

—**LeMarcus Newman**, NFL alumni, Mentor.org, Black Enterprise Top Modern Man of the Year

"In order to achieve the results that we are looking for in life, it requires us to shift our habits. Ahmard is one of those thought leaders who knows how to "move the ball" and can effectively motivate, inspire, and empower others to make the necessary changes to lead a fulfilling life. *Now What?* is a book filled with incredible insights and is a must read!"

—**Jen Garrett**, Author of *Move the Ball* and Host of the
Move the Ball Podcast

NOW WHAT

**5 Steps
to Get Up
and Create
the Most
of Life**

AHMARD MOORE VITAL

NEW YORK

LONDON • NASHVILLE • MELBOURNE • VANCOUVER

Now What

5 Steps to Get Up and Create the Most of Life

Published in New York, New York, by Morgan James Publishing. Morgan James is a trademark of Morgan James, LLC. www.MorganJamesPublishing.com

Proudly distributed by Ingram Publisher Services.

THE HOLY BIBLE, NEW INTERNATIONAL VERSION®, NIV® Copyright © 1973, 1978, 1984, 2011 by Biblica, Inc.® Used by permission. All rights reserved worldwide

Morgan James
BOGO™

A **FREE** ebook edition is available for you
or a friend with the purchase of this print book.

CLEARLY SIGN YOUR NAME ABOVE

Instructions to claim your free ebook edition:
1. Visit MorganJamesBOGO.com
2. Sign your name CLEARLY in the space above
3. Complete the form and submit a photo
   of this entire page
4. You or your friend can download the ebook
   to your preferred device

ISBN 9781631959219 paperback
ISBN 9781631959226 ebook
Library of Congress Control Number:
2022934495

Cover & Interior Design by:
Christopher Kirk
www.GFSstudio.com

Morgan James PUBLISHING
Builds
with...
Habitat for Humanity®
Peninsula and
Greater Williamsburg

Morgan James is a proud partner of Habitat for Humanity Peninsula
and Greater Williamsburg. Partners in building since 2006.

Get involved today! Visit MorganJamesPublishing.com/giving-back

Dedication

To The One

Table of Contents

So Much Gratitude...

Wow, there are so many to thank when it relates to this book coming together in this moment.

First, I want to thank my two fathers, the late Harry Vital and Melvin Moore, two men whose names I proudly bear and grace the cover of this book. Thank you both for you love, support and wisdom that I am grateful for as I embark on this journey called life.

To my family, the foundation needed for this project to come together. My mother Bernadette, brothers Onazeen and Eti. Sister Andrea, brother-in-law Kenneth and nephew and niece Kemahl and Keiarra. Also love for my baby niece Kassidi and son Jayden.

Thank you to my publisher Morgan James and David Hancock for seeing my vision for *Now What*. To my editor Sharon Mignerey, who gave my words life. Also, thanks to Keri Thoele and Mike and Alissa Brady for their editing assistance.

I'm grateful for the contributors to the book in Pastor Josh Pierce, Hjörtur Smarason, Cyrus Webb, Christopher Alan Zook, Dr. Greg Reid, Larisa Miller, and Reverend Jesse Jennings. Your words and wisdom brought added value to each chapter.

Thanks to all the mentors, coaches, pastors, ministers, teachers, professors, colleagues, and associates who have poured into me with your wisdom and strategies. I'm indebted to all of you. To my supporters and clients who have been with me since I was a ten dollar an hour sportswriter.

Most of all, thank you to my Lord and Savior Jesus Christ, who truly makes all things possible. Your words and walk are the great example, the fuel from which I draw strength each day. You are the key to all my success.

Introduction

You have picked up this book because you're looking for something. Maybe you are at a crossroads. Maybe you're at the end of a painful breakup. Maybe you are looking for answers to keep you from going down the same old path where you end up with the same old results. And just as the title says, "Now what?" I believe this book can help you with whatever you want next in your life by offering concrete suggestions and strategies that work. How do I know? Because they have worked for me.

You may have experienced an interesting upbringing that plays into why marriages or committed relationships result in separation of some kind. I have lived through this more than once, with a bevy of emotions. At times I handled the tumult well and other times, not so much. Regardless of the erroneous thoughts and actions I engaged in over the years, I was always striving to learn. I believe I'm a better man because of both the missteps and the learning. No matter where you may fall on the spectrum of fulfilling relationships and family, there is a new day ahead. Follow me on a quick recap on when constant negativity resulted in a great blessing.

If I were to say that the relationship between my biological father (Mr. Moore) and I was complicated, that would not give it proper justice. Perhaps many of you have a checkered or complicated past with your parents or guardians as well.

My parents divorced when I was ten years old, and almost immediately, my life as I knew it changed. My father was still working out of the country, and I was making monthly trips to my grandparents' home as written in the court order. I was not particularly fond of this, and my actions showed it. Anger, disgust, and outright insubordination were occurring every month. By age twelve I'd had enough, and I was no longer making these visits. At the time, I didn't realize these experiences would become the source of my work ethic and a foundation for strength as I became an adult. The turning point came in the autumn of 2004 as I was about to graduate from college.

With only fourteen hours remaining before I was to receive a bachelor's degree, my birth father agreed to meet with me. We had not spoken to one another in six years. He and my mother had worked out their differences in the court-room years prior, but their strained relationship left me with a lot of unanswered questions. For decades I had only heard one side of the story. Something within me always wanted to get his side of the story as well. During those adolescent years, I did have a father figure (Mr. Vital) in house as my mother had remarried. Thankfully, I was not lacking discipline, structure or responsibility while growing up; however, I still wanted to know why things hadn't work out between my biological father and my mother.

With graduation day approaching, I extended an olive branch to my birth father who was living overseas at the time. His P.O. box had been the same for many years with his mail forwarded to his residence in Africa. I sent out a graduation invitation to him, anticipating he would congratulate me via mail. After all, it had been many years since we had spoken by phone or in person. So, it came as a shock to me when I got an email from him the week of graduation. He acknowledged that he received the invitation, and though it was going to be tough, he would do everything in his power to make it to my graduation.

Two thoughts went through my head at that moment. One, I was glad to finally be done with school after nearly seven years in undergrad. And two, I may be able to get some face time with my dad and get some answers to those unanswered questions I had been thinking about for years.

Friday night before graduation, he sent me another email with his hotel information and phone number. I called him and said that I wanted to meet, suggesting a place I'd worked,

Bullfrogs, a popular sports bar in Nacogdoches, Texas near the Stephen F. Austin State University campus. He showed up and we ordered a round, Greyhound for him and Wild Turkey and Coke for me. A cordial conversation ensued, and we were able to clear the air about a few misconceptions we had over the years.

The question of "why" came up a lot as I recalled key moments in life, where I felt as though things were stacked against me. I have to admit I was being selfish in my questioning to him. My goal was for him to fill in the blanks of the incomplete stories of my life. For twenty years only one side had been shared. The conversation, which went on for hours and five to six rounds of drinks, was going well. Many of the answers I longed for were clarified. In some instances, I was shocked by the back story of how some stories played out behind the scenes.

At this point, the father/son connection was going well and starting to create some needed planks on the bridge of recovery. Still, I needed to present the question that was tugging on my heart all night, and possibly for the past five years. And that question was... why?

"Why were you gone so much? Why so detached over all those years? Why did we not spend more time together? Why did you only come home two to three times a year? Why did we rarely connect?"

The questions beginning with why continued vigorously, so much that it brought out a few tears (not a good look from a man who works in a sports bar).

I could tell that my dad was in deep thought, taking in all that I was saying. After I unloaded twenty-five years' worth of grievances and baggage, my father confidently turned to me and said the two words that resonated with me for the next fifteen years—right up to today.

"Now what?"

You can imagine the look on my face, and I'm thinking, "Dude, that's all you got?" After all that you shared with me, this is your response? I was stunned and perplexed. Was this an adequate answer to all of the questions I had asked of him? At the time, I thought no. It took me years to understand how wrong I was.

I now realize the relevance to my father's simple (but not simplistic) answer. And the truth is, he was right. For years I felt wronged, deprived, and neglected. That is the message I had told myself for nearly twenty years. My dad asked me, "What do you plan to do now, in this very moment?" Even if all my assessments were right, what could be changed presently? Right now, what am I going to do with my life going forward?

Now what? A bold truth, which came days later, hit me like a mental freight train. With a full deck of cards on the table, with everything from the past still in the past, I realized in the current moment that nothing can be done to change any of it. Essentially, my dad allowed me to purge all of those thoughts of resentment, which allowed me to hear myself in real time. Now a decision had to be made. That's when the "Now What" moment happened. As I say, I did not fully realize or appreciate how momentous that exchange was. However, the "Now what?" question became foundational to my growth and the man I am today.

The effects of choices and actions from the past have consequences that manifest in our current experience, and they shape how we operate now. These prior actions may even define us, but this is by our own choice. The ideology we carry forward from past trauma or disappointment does not have to define us and is not the end of the story. In all honesty, we're doing ourselves a disservice if this is the hill we choose to rest on. In the years since that discussion with my birth father, I see this was a moment of ruthless, yet beautiful clarity.

This project was born in that moment, and I am grateful for it. "Now What?" It's always and forever about "now." The only time we have is now. The past is already marked off the calendar. The future is not guaranteed. A new life philosophy was created when I experienced all of this. This has been the springboard I use to enhance my business and professional life, as well as my personal life.

"Now What" is an invitation to take an intense look at your past challenges in life, identify what was beneficial and sift through the positives within your experiences. The benefits are there and there are plenty of them. When those two words came to me on that Friday evening so long ago, it got me thinking. What can I do, today, right now, to create a better life? And then it hit me as five strategies came to mind while processing ways to maximize the good presently in my life.

REFLECT

When you reflect on where you are now, you may be tempted to play the blame game and point fingers at others for your current state of affairs. This is counterproductive, and your energy is better suited in other ways. Reflection allows you to evaluate those experiences to the insight needed to use what was beneficial while releasing the negative aspects. Harboring negative thoughts will produce more of its kind.

DECIDE

There can be no change until a decision is made. When faced with a challenge that you need to overcome, you can choose to be a victim or a doer. Clearly, the choice is the latter when working towards something greater in value. Making a decision is an important first step to a better life. Without bold decisions, you are destined to remain on the same well-worn path with its familiar ruts. It's likely if you are reading this, the same is no longer sufficient for your long- or short-term goals. Decide to overcome the mental trap of drifting through life hoping things will happen. Look in the mirror and own your current life by releasing the unwanted fears that you've carried for years. Only then can you move forward towards a specific end.

PLAN

If you have no plan, all you have is a wish. Progress will be a difficult and uphill journey. Life, especially one with a purpose, is already littered with roadblocks. A lack of planning will postpone your goals into an uncertain someday. Having a blueprint of where you want to move forward with your life is key to achieving your goals. Plans enable you to create a clear vision of the person you want to be, the things you want to do, and the beautiful life you want to have.

ACT

Action is the fuel of creation. The longer you sit and ponder on what should be done, the longer your goals sit dormant. No movement means no change, and no change creates nothing (as in no thing). Goals on paper are a plan, but plans require action. Plans without action turn goals from dreams into unfulfilled blessings. It's always in the doing that gets it done professionally and personally. Nothing moves if you choose to not make moves.

SEEK

No one reaches success alone. This is mentioned several times throughout the book but cannot be shared enough. The most successful people seek out experts, information, skills, and strategies to help them reach their goals each day. There is no one-man show. Seeking counsel on your journey to make your goals shift from idea to reality requires the help of others. Seek for all that you need, be humble in acquiring it and be grateful for it.

CLOSING

Within the pages of this book, prepare for the challenge, with pen and paper in hand. My dad may not have known that he awakened something in me. After that night, I was better able to look at life through an objective lens, which is invaluable. When you awaken each morning, show gratitude for where you are, regardless of the circumstances. If you take an honest look at your life, you've already accomplished something of value, no matter how insignificant it may seem to you. Start by building on that. Accept responsibility for your life as you plan your next steps.

The proper question is that simple one I was asked all those years ago. Now What?

Chapter 1:

Reflect

Def: to think deeply, especially about possibilities and values

"Your reflection is a collection of choices and challenges."

AFFIRMATION: "As I enter into the moment of reflection, I affirm that I have increasing clarity about my life, including all that I want to be, do, and have."

REFLECT TO REVEAL

You may be tempted to see your reflection as the real you. It is true a mirror that can only reflect what it is given, but the reflection is still a snapshot of how you are right now. Part of taking stock is that unflinching look, but an equal part of it is beginning to imagine what is possible. We are all familiar with the meme of a kitten looking into a mirror to the majestic lion looking back. As you reflect on where you currently are, you see the culmination of your life's experiences to this point. That's all. Now, like that kitten seeing a lion, you can begin to envision all the possibilities. Whatever the reflection reveals to you, it is filled with both negatives (the things you want to eliminate or improve) and positives (the strengths and talents that will carry you forward). These two things give back the image that is facing it, experiences, and possibilities. From a mental standpoint, reflection is an important aspect of life.

Reflection allows you to see the challenges, the wins, the journey, and what was learned and gained. Everything that happened in your life, whether by choice or happenstance, is not time lost. It is part of your larger journey.

Imagine that success is an ongoing experiment, with you as the primary subject. Your choices and experiences produce results, favorable or unfavorable. Either way, those are learning, teachable moments. Consider this: perhaps those past occurrences prepared you for the moments that are happening right now. What if those experiences gave you the mental toughness to build the confidence you need now to make new, bold, and empowered changes needed to enhance your life? In this, you are already a success, even if not by the standards someone else may have set for you.

All the mental tools needed for this now moment are the results of past choices and results. Right now, it's likely that you are better prepared than you realize due the consequential effects from the past. Poets and musicians have long written about the mistakes we all make along the way and how we learn from them whether poetically put, like Carl Sandburg's "The broken boulders by the road shall not commemorate my ruin" or Kanye West's lament about his wrongs being the creative source for writing a song about those wrongs from his hit song, *Touch the Sky.*

The tough moments serve as a warning signal to proceed with caution. Conversely, when used properly, a warning signal also gives you the fuel to press on. You know your struggle. You also know your threshold and breaking points as you have been tested in the past. Now, you are ready to play a bigger game with fortitude and confidence.

Your next steps are empowered as a result reflecting on all that you have lived through, regardless of how you labeled it, success, or failure. Later in this chapter you will start the process of imagining your chosen future. In this imagining, you are beginning to design your life. You have reflected on where you are now, including the strengths you want to build on and the bad habits to be released. You have envisioned what you want to be, and you are ready to create. That's right, you are ready to be an artist (more on that later).

EYES ON YOUR PAPER

Remember your school days when the teacher said, "keep your eyes on your own paper?"

He or she may have intended this to be a deterrent to cheating. In fact, this has a more important meaning: focus on what you're doing. Many times, you may have the urge to compare the success of others to your own. When you are first working towards something new and exciting to improve your life, it's your own vision that matters. Looking at your progress in a pessimistic way leads to resentment and envy. The degree of success another achieves has nothing to do with your own. So, that teacher's advice is sound. Keep your eyes on your own paper.

When you do look at that other person's success and prosperity, see it with this in mind. How did they achieve success, and what steps did they take to operate on this level? The study of habits, actions and mindset utilized by others to achieve can be valuable. Study without comparing, then adopt what is helpful to your own journey. Success leaves clues, and taking down a few notes from successful people can be of great benefit.

You may use the excuse of "no one believed in me" to justify your current situation. It's probably true that you had teachers or others who constantly reminded you that success would not be in your future and that you will amount to little to nothing. Do you really believe that for your entire life that no one ever believed that you would become successful? Those words may have bruised your ego, but what if those words had hidden value – though not always ideal – to push you to your true potential and used as a tool of motivation?

More often than not, adversity is the fuel for your potential. To illustrate: As a preteen, my parents got divorced, and it was not a good time in my life (separation never is). After my mother remarried, adjusting to my new father also had its complications. In addition, I had teachers who weren't keen on the idea that I would ever become successful. Without knowing why at the time, I focused on those who did see my potential. I gravitated to those who gave me second chances, even when I was out of line, reckless and making dumb, adolescent choices.

In high school, Ms. Keri Thoele helped me perfect my English skills and fine-tuned my writing, while Mr. Alex Carillo gave me the firm foundation with an opportunity in journalism. Coaches Tim Smith and Chris Nelson maximized my athletic talents which led to a short stint on a Division I football team. Once I enrolled at Stephen F. Austin State, Dr. Gary Mayer stressed the idea of ethics in journalism while Dr. Deanne Malpass taught me the proper way to effectively study and prepare for the tests of life. If you take a closer look at your own life and accomplishments, it's likely that you have mentors you may not have recognized at the time. Remember them. Acknowledge them. Be grateful for them. Progress of any kind is possible when you accept the fact that there is always information that you know you don't know. Mentors, other support members in your life, can make a huge impact in you achieving your goals. Hold on to this idea as the Seek chapter expounds on this further.

EAT YOUR GUMBO

It's no secret. At some point in life, you have fallen short of reaching the goals. It happens because as a human you have flaws.

With every flaw, mistake, problem caused, mishap and wrong decision, there is a major opportunity. Question, how do you view all that you have been through? Do you focus on the mishaps or the opportunities?

When I host events throughout the year, my sister often makes a large pot of gumbo, a family favorite. It tastes the same from one time to the next, but it's also different. Each time I consume it, I enjoy a new element within this delicious dish. My sister told me that her gumbo includes flour, olive oil, okra, celery, tomatoes, sausage, chicken, onions, shrimp, broth, garlic, bell peppers and a host of other goodies.

When you look at the totality of the gumbo recipe, it's evident that there is a lot going that exceeds the qualities of any individual ingredient. This is much like you. Within you, there are many hidden elements, gifts, talents, and layers that exceed their individual qualities.

Your experiences are a culmination of your challenges and opportunities. Some experiences you are proud of while others not so much. You, like that large pot of gumbo, are a mixture of emotions, good and bad decisions, values, regrets, and triumphs.

You may or may not be proud of how you've lived life to this point. You may even be ashamed. But yet, here you are.

Maybe you have children who can't stand the sight of you, an ex-spouse who wants you dead or an extended family that stopped inviting you to outings years ago.

For today, enjoy your gumbo with all of its variety, knowing there may be some uncomfortable and unwanted contents within it. Your own recipe can be adjusted to help you face what you do not like while also adding the good items that are simmered within your pot of life. Your life, like that gumbo recipe, can be changed for the better.

SEE IT, FEEL IT

Pray. Meditate. Daydream.

A clear, relaxed mind helps you to have a clear perception. Any of the following mind-body connecting exercises will work to clear your mind. Within you there is a bigger, tougher, more insightful version of you. Sometimes you just need to disconnect from the everyday, immediate concerns. This intentional silent time will be beneficial for you. Below is a simple meditation.

Go to a quiet place – indoors or outdoors – and tune out as much outside noise (sometimes the sound of nature is a good thing, though planes and trains, not so much) as possible. Sit comfortably.

Close your eyes. Take in deep breaths, inhaling for a four-second count and then exhale. Do this five times and then sit still.

After taking in the breaths, remain in stillness. The objective here is to clear your mind, taking it off of everything. Simply be in the moment. Take in another breath. To encourage your mind to become quiet, say softly to yourself, "Breathe" as you release the breath. Repeat this for five minutes. If you cannot do five minutes, begin with a minute, and work up to three, five, and eventually fifteen minutes.

To expand on this simple meditation, add another word in between "breathe." This might be a word that focuses your mind on something you want, such as "calm," "peace," or some other word (a single syllable works best) that is meaningful to you.

Another addition to this practice is to have in mind a question that you would like an answer to when you begin meditation. Write down the question. Then let go of the question while you meditate. When you are finished meditating, write down any thoughts or insights that emerge immediately after you're done.

WHO TOLD YOU THAT?

The opening chapter of the Bible has a passage that relates a conversation between God and Adam.

But the Lord God called to the man, and said to him, "Where are you?" He said, "I heard the sound of you in the garden, and I was afraid, because I was naked; and I hid myself." He said, "Who told you that you were naked? Have you eaten from the tree of which I commanded you not to eat?"

This story illustrates a deep-rooted mental conundrum that many face on a daily basis. Here is a committed couple, united by God in Adam and Eve, living in the garden (of Eden) carefree. As the story is told, the man and woman are on land where they have access to everything they need to live a glorious and prosperous life. All that was asked of them was to not eat from a particular tree. After Eve, ate of the tree, she gave the fruit to Adam. Their carefree feelings turned into nervousness and negation. So naturally, when God called on them, they attempted to hide, ashamed of what they had done. The idea of anything negative about them had not been introduced, not once. This change in mindset, which was once positive and pure in quality, led to choices that resulted in a lack of trust, selfishness, and loss of property.

The moral of this story is your negative thoughts about yourself came from some outside source. Meaning, you were not born with negative thoughts or a toxic self-image. These were learned, which means they can be unlearned. So, when you decide to embark on a new journey in life to, make meaningful changes, beware of those thoughts of lack and unworthiness that will prevent you from achieving your goals.

I remember coaching a young man back in the day who had made a few mistakes that led to some serious setbacks. During one of our sessions, he said something that I'll never forget.

"You gotta understand. I ain't sh-t, and I ain't ever gonna be sh-t."

Somewhere within his life he must have heard plenty of this negative talk, and the danger is this had become the truth to him. Doubting yourself hinders you from making moves because of fear, and that fear results in a lack of belief in yourself can be debilitating.

Maybe you know where your negative ideas came from and maybe not. Parents, a teacher, someone of authority, or even someone whom you trusted implanted these harmful ideas into your subconscious. Becoming aware of them is step one to eliminating them.

UNPACK AND PURGE

For you to process the many ideas that flow through you daily, a clear mind is needed. As my mentor often said, "Your outer reality is a reflection of your inner world." I took that literally, and I found that when I had a clear, organized workspace, my mind was also clearer and more organized.

My mentor's rationale was simple. When your physical surroundings are cluttered, your ability to think effectively is also cluttered. Several psychological studies, including one published in the Journal of Environmental Psychology (June 2016) identify that clutter – defined as "an overabundance of possessions that collectively create chaotic and disorderly living spaces" – and a disorganized working and living environment affects your overall mental health.

To test this for yourself, clean and declutter your workspace to get rid of unwanted things so your mind has fewer distractions. This all makes physical and mental space for the next game-changing idea that arises. Identify for yourself how your mentality matches your physical surroundings.

Canadian clinical psychologist Jordan Peterson states in *12 Rules for Life*, that you need to clean your room first before you can take on larger more complex challenges in life. Meaning, you can start with what seems like a small task of cleanliness, so your immediate space is in order. A clear space makes for a clear head, and clear head is the foundation for generating new ideas.

FORGIVE ME...

In many instances the brick wall that stands between you and your transformation is regret and guilt. You are your own worst enemy. Do you realize that your mind cannot tell the difference between real and imagined experiences? You can demonstrate this by imagining the death of someone you love; the feelings of loss and sadness that overcome you suggest this is real. So, the regret and guilt you feel about past mistakes can be as intense now as when the event causing them happened. The weight on your mental shoulders can be a heavy burden to bear.

Forgiveness of others and yourself is often an ongoing process before it frees you from the clutches of guilt, shame, and regret. You know you've made progress when you can remember the hurtful event or person without your emotions being triggered. This work is essential and at times messy. Forgiveness leads to freedom.

Releasing thoughts of being a victim is the elephant in the room. To release this mentality, it must be faced head on, internally. In the book *Radical Forgiveness*, author Colin C. Tipping encourages everyone to face their victimhood head on and embrace the experiences to work towards a healthy transformation.

To put into practice, create a hit list of immoral acts encountered, along with the people involved in the moment. After you make the list, which may have brought up emotions you don't want, set aside time to go through these items, one by one, perhaps choosing the easiest one first. Identify your beliefs or behaviors that may have either directly contributed to what happened or put you in a position of being taken advantage of. Were you too timid or too trusting, which put you in harm's way? Were you mouthy or disrespectful when silence would have served you better? This is part of the unflinching assessment that can be very uncomfortable.

Then, identify strengths you have today that you would have not had if you had not gone through this experience. Are you more confident, more empathetic about the pain others feel, more willing to intervene if you see someone else being wronged? Since this is part of you now, it is important to recognize how this experience contributes to the kind of person you have become.

Make no mistake. This is a difficult process, but you will find more peace and more strength on the other side.

NEVER QUIT

You have the freedom to choose the opportunities you want to pursue. Along the way, you will encounter obstacles, setbacks, financial constraints, and adversities. When you pursue something new and valuable, you may struggle and fail many times before seeing any sign of progress, much less success. With that, you may be tempted to give up. Failure is a natural part of life as you aim to pursue worthwhile goals. Most of the time failure has less to do with your physical characteristics and more to do with your choices.

Mindset is the starting point of everything. The results of your life are placed squarely on your shoulders. Start your day, every day, with a focus on, "What can I do today to make my life better?" Take your mind off "what is not," and focus on "what is." The "what is" invites you to open the gift of life, which is in the present moment.

3G APPROACH

Reflection on what you have going at the moment is positive even though you have probably discovered things you don't like. This gives you something to build upon: healthy thoughts of appreciation. These thoughts are beneficial as you focus on the skills, expertise and beneficial work that needs to be invested in your new endeavors. When you take an honest look at your life, there is plenty of good already occurring, regardless of how far off the success path you feel you are.

To recognize the good in your life, practicing gratitude (more on this later) is a foundational necessity. When you awaken each morning, here is a quick exercise that brings appreciation into sharp focus called the 3G Approach.

To begin, start with a composition book or a journal or notebook that has at least eighty full sized pages so you can fit your entire entry on one line. Keep your notebook on your nightstand or somewhere near your bedside. You want this to be within easy reach since this will be one of the first items you use each morning.

When you awaken and your feet hit the floor, with each step, tell yourself, "Thank You." At this moment, your mind will go into action, processing why you claimed those two words as the first words out of your mouth every morning.

With your book nearby, grab it out and write down three entries:

I am grateful that I… (two entries of gratitude of any kind)

My goal for today is… (one goal you want to accomplish that day)

This daily 3G Approach is a simple, yet effective way to begin your day with positivity and focus. Repeat this daily until it becomes habitual. The purpose is to begin your day on a higher mental playing field. You'll want to do this exercise within five minutes of waking up. These thoughts need to be fresh, out of your head and onto paper. This simple exercise keeps you from bringing yesterday's troubles into a new day and keeps gratitude at the front of your mind. Study after study reveals that people who achieve at a high level have in common one thing: a daily habit of gratitude.

Once you have these three statements written, repeat each of them aloud three times to yourself. This may seem weird at first as you are talking to yourself, and that's true because you are, but remember you are working with your subconscious mind. Thinking your affirmations, then writing, seeing, speaking, and hearing them is a mental exercise. This five-step process activates your senses, which will jump start your day on a positive note. This may feel strange early on, but trust in knowing that your mind must be conditioned and used properly for maximum results.

If you have one of those days where you think you have nothing to be grateful for, look to the smallest things possible around you. You may be grateful for a warm, dry bed. You may be grateful to have made it through a night. You may be grateful simply for awaking. Your goals may be equally small. The point of the exercise is to find two things to be grateful for, no matter how small and to find one goal, no matter how small. The axiom is true that the longest journey begins with that small, first step. Begin right where you are.

Commit to this practice each day. Treat this as something as important as breakfast, grooming and your shower. This is fitness for your mind. It will thank you and you'll be on your way to a better day every day.

Final Thoughts on Reflection with Pastor Josh Pierce

Moments of Reflection Lead to a Solid Foundation

How important has taking time to reflect been to your overall successes?

Honestly, I have painstakingly learned the value of reflection. It's not something that comes naturally to me. When I'm alone with my thoughts, I have no problem processing the upcoming plan in an attempt to see the angles of what's about to happen, but reflection used to feel like a waste of time. Why would I want to look back? Where was the value in thinking through something that already happened when

I was powerless to change it? If I reflect on a tough situation, I'm just holding on to it and that's not healthy. Thoughts like those were my rationale for not taking the time to reflect on the good, the bad, and the ugly… and I'm sad to say that I regret the long portion of my life in my 20's when I almost refused to 'think back' while convincing myself that only the best leaders 'think forward.' I finally started to realize there might be a better way, but only after I was paying a high price.

As I struggled to reflect, I couldn't see how God was helping me to grow because I was always focused on the next step. Then, I would beat myself up about not being good enough to already be at the 'next step,' instead of celebrating where God had brought me from in a relatively short amount of time. It's a good lesson to learn… when you don't celebrate what God has done and how far you've come, you are (by default) not praising Him for those things either. It took me several years of hard work and accountability to retrain my brain and my heart to recognize the value of purposeful reflection, but now that I'm able to pause and reflect on the big (and small) things in life, I am able to properly learn from my mistakes, celebrate what God is doing, and chart a better course for the future.

What specific project or accomplishment in particular was taking a moment to reflect most imperative to you and those whom you lead?

Sometimes you have to look back to look forward. In 2015, I was having a hard time trying to figure out what God had planned for my future in ministry. Thankfully, I had many options professionally, but the lack of clarity around my purpose and calling was causing me to pause before I made any decisions. On one hand, I was at peace with where God had me. But on the other hand, I couldn't shake the feeling that He might be moving me into a new season. A pivotal moment in this journey was when my wife told me, "You should just get away for a night to think and pray about what God wants from us." I took her advice and booked a hotel room about thirty minutes away from where we lived… a beautiful tourist destination called Park City, Utah. With a gorgeous mountain view outside my hotel window, I spent most of the night thinking, praying, singing, and writing. I allowed myself to take a deep dive into the memories of planting a church years before, and I reflected on the lessons I had learned, people I had poured into, and people that had poured into me. As I looked back on how God had been shaping my life, how my family had grown, and how I had been stretched, my vision for the future was actually becoming more clear. In other words, the more I reflected on what had happened… the more I understood what could happen. Sometimes you have to look back to look forward.

How would you advise someone who maybe has been reluctant in sitting still and taking time to reflect, not seeing this as an important aspect of life?

There are lots of reasons why someone might feel reflection is difficult… it's boring and tedious… it's too painful… it's not worth the effort… life is too busy… etc. If you have bought into one (or all) of these excuses, I would urge you to first and foremost reconsider your thinking. If you want to take big steps, do great things, engage in dynamic relationships, raise wonderful children, build important companies, and lead yourself and your family well, you must spend high-quality time reflecting on what has worked, what hasn't worked, and what God taught you through the process. If you never reflect, you will keep making the same mistakes over and over again. If you never reflect, you'll struggle to see how far you've come. It's not easy... but it's worth it.

In addition to investing time to reflect, what is another important principle that was used in conjunction with reflecting that has been beneficial to your success?

The most difficult person to lead is yourself. Reflection, just like many other things in life, should develop into a personal discipline. There should be moments carved out in your life... your year, your month, your week, and even your day... to spend purposeful time in reflection. But even if you get a nudge from someone to make it happen (your boss, spouse, friend, coach, etc.), you still have to internalize the value of it and set yourself up for success. You have to lead yourself to be able to set aside precious time... on a regular basis... without distraction. If you are an 'achiever' personality, or if you are pretty sure you have ADHD, you might have some trouble slowing down enough to make it happen. But again, just like working out, eating right, and reading your Bible... it must become a non-negotiable discipline in your life. Why?

Because reflection builds on itself. Just one time of 'pausing your life to reflect' might not make that big of a difference, but a couple of minutes per day, or a day per month, or a week per year, will establish momentum and depth in your thinking that can't happen without purpose and structure. So do the hard work of leading yourself to make it a pattern… a routine… a non-negotiable discipline in your life.

Please share some parting words for those who needed an added push and words of encouragement to begin pursuing their life goals with a sense of purpose.

Four simple words for you… I believe in you. Have you had those words spoken to you recently? If not, read it again… I believe in you. We all need to hear it from time to time. If you are reading this valuable book, you are already taking some first steps necessary to pursue your goals with purpose. But when it gets difficult to pursue your dreams (and I promise it will get difficult…), remember that you have people around you that will support you and cheer you on… get around those people as much as you can. Be around people who believe in you and what you are capable of. But also run from those people who tear you down, distract you, or cause you to stumble or doubt what God has called you to do.

Trust me, when you have incredible people in your corner who believe in you, it makes a world of difference. Then… and this is my favorite part of the cycle… when you have accomplished some of what you have set out to do, you'll be able to look at someone who is just starting out and declare the same thing with experience and conviction... I believe in you.

Bio: Josh Pierce was born into a ministry family and has been in full-time ministry for eighteen years. After serving as the Youth Pastor to over 300 teenagers in Green Bay, WI, he and his wife, Brooke, moved to Salt Lake City, UT in 2007 to help plant City Church and served in a variety of pastoral roles as the church grew. In June of 2016, Josh and his family moved to Houston, TX to become the Executive Pastors at Grace Woodlands. Josh loves to lead worship, read, teach, and help develop young leaders and pastors. He and Brooke have been married for sixteen years, and they have two amazing sons – Landon and Nathan.

Pastor Josh's contact information is available on the Grace Woodlands website at www.gracewoodlands.com

Chapter 2:
Decide

Def: come to a mental resolution about a topic as a result of reflection

AFFIRMATION: In this moment, I am confident that I make decisions that empower and enhance me as I move closer to my goals and dreams. I affirm this truth today.

VALUE OF WHY

But first, coffee right? Wrong.

First why? Then coffee.

In the last chapter, we explored the need to reevaluate your life, especially if it seems aimless where you drift from one mundane task to another. Life, to have any feeling of fulfillment, needs purpose. One of the best ways to remain motivated through building and creating your better life is to know your why. When your "why" is not clearly defined, you lack sound reasons that support the tasks you do on a daily basis.

Remember being a kid asking the why questions? Why do I have to go to school? Why is grass green and the sky blue? Why do ships float and rocks sink? As you grew older, your why questions probably became more personal. Why didn't I get the grade I wanted on a test? And, as you became an adult, maybe your why questions got harder. Why do I want to go to college at a particular school or why do I want to grow my business a particular way? The longing you have to become something more than you are today is expressed through the answer to "why do I want that?"

The essence of why is intrinsic. It's a longing which happens within you, helping you to operate without outside influences or motivation. It merges the connection between your purpose and mission. "Why" is the fuel for your deepest lifelong achievements. Scottish theologian William Barclay said, "There are two great days in a person's life: the day we are born and the day we discover why." Truth is many people maneuver through life without ever knowing their why.

Discovering your why is not an easy task. It is an inner yearning that that requires intense work. The effort to identify your why can be challenging. As English writer Agatha Christie wrote in her detective fiction, *Five Little Pigs*, "For some the why comes easily and for others not so much. 'Ah, but my dear sir, the why must never be obvious. That is the whole point.'" With that said, here is a crash course to embody your why so you may live life with more fulfillment and purpose.

This example comes courtesy of Simon Sinek, co-author of *Find Your Why*. To_____ so that_____.

The first blank is for the contribution you plan to give to the world, while the second blank is for the impact that the stated contribution will bring to the world. Feel free to play around with this and find the combination that works best for you.

As an example, here's one I created:

"To <u>inspire and empower communities worldwide</u> so that <u>future generations will see empowering examples of success, knowing it's possible for them also</u>."

Remember this declarative statement is unique to you. After you have thought this through and have established this proclamation for yourself, know that "why" goes far greater than what you do. It combines what you do, who you are and what cause you want to address. This bold statement becomes a way of life that is attached to you no matter the setting.

Your why is the energetic, full-of-life sensation that follows you to work, church, your place of business, the grocery store, your kid's ball game or the gym. Have you ever heard someone say, "there's just something about (fill in name here)?" Perhaps you have heard this about yourself already. This is an element of your why in action.

Taking time to discover the meaning to your life takes introspection. Time alone with your thoughts has intrinsic value that helps you discover how to accept, own, and live your why on a daily basis. You may connect your "why" to family. You might embrace the idea of bringing life into this world. You might feel that the grooming, raising, and teaching of young people has value so your legacy will continue. You may embrace social causes, such as sustainable clean water, addressing the homeless epidemic, lessoning world hunger worldwide or addressing poverty in the inner cities. Whatever you choose will have its foundation in your why.

I absolutely love what I do. While I work, teach, and consult in a business and philanthropic capacity, my heart and soul are into investing and empowering young adults (aged fifteen to twenty-seven). This is the prime age when young adults are seeking guidance to prepare for adulthood. Many of them are stuck at the crossroads between information overload, and how to properly use this information to build a solid foundation for success in life. One key factor for them is the challenge of figuring out, "what do I want to do with my life?" My life is committed to helping them sift through the available information, putting together a plan so they may take their first step on their life's path. For me, it comes down to working daily to become the man I needed in my own life when I was seventeen, which means I must continue to hone my knowledge and skills.

The importance of why brings greater meaning on how you spend your time, what thoughts emerge daily, and how you organize your schedule.

FROM CHALLENGE TO RESULT

There will always be a challenge ahead of you, whether you choose to pursue a goal or not. Question, is why you would not take on new challenges since they are opportunities in disguise awaiting your pursuit? The challenge can be big or small, it does not matter. Overcoming them can still provide you with a means to do more for your family and yourself. What could possibly be holding you up? Here are a few things that may be hindering you from making the decision to pursue your goals.

Stagnation

Even when things are great, good, or perhaps okay, a life overall can become stale when goals lose their newness, or are set on a back burner, and the drudgery of an uninspired routine sets in.

If you find yourself in this place, actively decide to overcome stagnation no matter how tough to overcome. One way to break out of this is to speak with a coach or mentor to help you unpack the issues you may have. An outside, trusted voice can listen to all that you have going on and can often provide a new perspective or a simple solution that you weren't able to see. Review your big "why" to see if it continues to inspire you.

Scatterbrained

When a new goal or project is first pursued, it is often filled with a ton of ideas, each one perhaps seeming equal in importance, which makes it tough to nail down the priorities. A person in this stage may jump from one task to another or forget important tasks.

If you find yourself being scatterbrained, actively decide to write down all your ideas to identify the pros, cons, importance, and cost of each. From there, you will be able to see which ones align with your values and priorities in life, and you will be able to rank them based on their relative value.

Transition

Pursing new goals can be uncomfortable and is rarely convenient. Waiting on the right time will result in the postponement of their fulfillment. People have all sorts of valid reasons from a bad break up, a death in the family, getting downsized or even bankruptcy. All of these are life changing and create a great deal of stress.

If you find yourself putting off your goals because you are in the middle of a transition, actively decide to flesh out your goals. What better time to begin than when you're in the middle of a transition?

Effects and Causes

When life happens (which it will), many people find themselves reacting to one stressful issue, then another. They may even recognize the same issues keep reoccurring.

If you find yourself always reacting to what life throws at you, actively decide to be proactive. That begins with having a heart-to-heart talk with yourself so you can recognize the mindset that causes these issues. This will allow you to release the behaviors that lead to self-sabotage so you can move forward.

YOU ARE CHOSEN (CALL TO OBEY)

Choosing your "why" is of utmost importance. And by doing so, you are ultimately making the choice to invest in yourself. For you to provide the best and bless others, you need to ensure you are bringing the best version of you to the table. Remember, you are able to give more when becoming more. You are deserving of all the best that life has to offer. Never forget that. Opportunities and possibilities are endless when you choose the best for you. Greater things are in store for you once you realize that you are indeed, a chosen one.

You might ask, chosen to do what? The short answer is whatever you desire. While there will be challenges involved and will take stages to accomplish to reach an intended goal, the path is all yours and your choice to activate.

Conversely, you may ask what happens when you decide to ignore your chosen duty, sometimes referred to as "obeying your calling." Remember purpose, your "why" is similar to a life mission. Once this mission is identified, it becomes a long-ing as its fulfillment becomes one of high importance. So, what happens when you ignore, or perhaps neglect this calling? Let's take a look at the age-old story of a man named Jonah.

As the Bible says, God called to Jonah to preach to Nineveh because the people were acting in an immoral way. Instead of taking heed to the purpose God called for him, he decided instead to take a boat to Tarshish. Because of his dis-obedience, God sent a storm upon the ship where Jonah was aboard. While the shipmen did attempt to veer away from the storm surge, the men came to the conclusion that perhaps Jonah was to blame, so they decided to throw him overboard. Once this happened, the storm was over.

Jonah was drowning. Then a big fish (a whale in some inter-pretations) was sent by God to swallow Jonah and to save him from drowning. Inside the belly the fish, Jonah called out for God and asked for forgiveness and prayed for help. For three days Jonah was in the belly of the fish. Interestingly enough, God had the fish throw up Jonah and he landed on the shores of Nineveh, the place where God had chosen for him to be.

Ironic huh? Jonah began preaching to the people Nineveh, warning them to atone before the city was set be destroyed in forty days. The people of Nineveh believed in Jonah and stopped their evil ways and sinful mindsets. God showed compassion to the people for the work that they and Jonah had accomplished. And though Jonah was angry at the divine assignment from God, he did indeed realize that he was chosen for this mission, and it was fulfilled.

What are you chosen to do? This is a question that may take significant time to answer. Your first answer may not be the one that leads you to pursuing a mission that exceeds your lifetime. Imagine what your life's purpose would look like. Do whatever it takes: visualize, daydream, meditate, prayer. Open your mind and activate your childlike faith with a wild imagination so you can have a snapshot of what your best life looks like.

ADDITION BY SUBTRACTION

For all those out there who have adopted some form of fitness, you know there are certain practices you need to ensure your mental and physical health. For this example, we will focus on the latter. Let's say that you lift weights and exercise three times a week, and for each session you burn anywhere from 500-800 calories, depending on intensity. For that to be effective in maintaining or losing weight, your caloric intake must be equal to or less than what your burn rate is. For an extreme example, you cannot have a nutritional plan where you take in 3,000 to 5,000 calories a day when you're expending fewer than that. The math simply does not add up. If this approach continues, it won't take long before you start seeing and feeling an increase in your waistline. Your body, much like your goals, is an investment and you will need to be disciplined in your habits in order to stay fit.

Compare this mindset to the goals you have in place. If a time and monetary investment is needed for the fulfillment of your goals, perhaps you need to hit pause on going to happy hour with friends on Fridays. Activities such as this one and other outings may need to happen less often going forward. If you and the family have four vacations planned for the year, maybe two will have to suffice for a couple of years.

The truth is that some events, actions, and people may not be part of your life during the season of your higher pursuit. Oh, did you catch that? "People" was indeed mentioned. And yes, some of them may not provide you value needed during this time in your life. Much like the example author Jon Gordon used in *The Energy Bus*, some people are Energy Vampires, people who bring an unhealthy dose of negativity with their presence. Making the choice to eliminate these negative influences in your life is not an easy decision. You are on the path of increase in your life, and with that means becoming and earning more. When you are committed to the journey of self-improvement, the value added by subtraction is a worthwhile one.

As with anything you choose to pursue, a mindset shift occurs. The mind is a chief factor in creating new and exciting things in your life. Say you found a company you would love to work for. It has a great product, stellar reputation and known for treating its customers and employees with great respect. You apply and get hired. Let's use the Enterprise Rental Car Corporation as an example.

The Enterprise company is known for promoting employees within its own system. Based on the company culture, which is well documented, the company stands by this philosophy. To start, an employee would begin with management trainee program. Then, through hitting performance and sales goals, would advance to management assistant then assistant manager to branch manager. This is the career path of opportunity that is afforded to those who are hired on. Once reaching the branch manager status, there are several career choices paths to follow, based on the goals of the employee. Area manager, HR, finance, and vice president/general manager are all viable options if one so chooses.

This illustration was laid out in a way to highlight the main idea, mindset matters. If you, as an Enterprise employee, want to continue advancing through promotions on a path to success, the opportunities are available. However, there is a catch. There is no path available for you to move from trainee to branch manager if your mind is still focused on being content in trainee mode. Meaning, you will need to study, think, and begin to embody a manager mindset to become one. Small thinking produces small results.

I had a mentor who once shared that he never had issues moving up the corporate ladder when he worked for a Fortune 500 company. His personal commitment was to complete the duties within his job description and produce an additional twenty to twenty-five percent above his normal responsibilities. He advises his clients to dress for the job they want, not the job they already had. He is teaching a shift in mindset, which creates habits and patterns. Whatever the next step in your life looks like, start at once to think, act, dress and operate in that manner.

In the movie *Boiler Room*, Jim Young, played by Ben Affleck, told the guys who were looking to become stock-brokers, to "Act

As If." While sparing you with the vulgarity of the scene, he told the guys to act like they were the big man on the block. He wanted them to look the part, act the part and dress the part, which ultimately will result in becoming the part. In short, he was encouraging them to embody a winning and dominant mindset.

This is not about a delusional and arrogant way to go about your business. Instead, it is a shift in consciousness and awareness within your outlook and confidence. It's a quest to becoming more of the person you seek to be. Make the decision to remove those limited thoughts and begin focusing on the strength you already have within so that you can become the greatest version of you and excel in life.

I AM (IT'S ALL MENTAL)

In the human language, there are no two more powerful words than "I Am." When these two words are spoken in an empowering way, they create, build, empower and inspire. Since the beginning of creation, even before recorded time, I Am has been the foundation of civilization. This is why in many interpretations regard IAM as divine. In this example, we will take it one step further and use I Am as an acronym for It's All Mental. As you decide what you want to build, create, or enhance, a strong and divine mental attitude is paramount.

Think about the foundational principles associated with "I Am." When you use these two words, whatever words that follows is what you declare about yourself. "I Am" (fill in the blank). Therefore, you want to choose your words carefully.

You want to use I Am as a proclamation, so your full statement becomes affirmative. Think about when you say, "I Am Awesome." That produces a natural energy flow that empowers you to become what you proclaim so it becomes truth. This must go beyond mere semantics and requires a multi-step process.

Prior to the verbalization of your chosen words, a thought (conscious or unconscious) has to occur. At that point, life has been spoken. The words spoken are then heard by you. Thinking, saying, and hearing are the first three steps, with the finale coming full circle making its way back to your mind where it originated. The "I Am" words are an essential life process that enhance or hinder your every-day routine. Choose your words wisely and respect the power of the "I Am," because those two words become the truth of who you are.

PURSUE VALUE

As you continue your quest in deciding who you want to become and what you want to do, pursue endeavors that produce value. Whether it is goods, services, or products, focus on who will benefit from what you provide. Do you have a solution to an ongoing challenge? Is what you are providing needed and necessary on the open and free market? Are you filling a void or enhancing someone's life experience with your service? These are important questions that need answers as you make decisions and press ahead.

One way to determine the value of what you plan to do is to study the market. People are always in search of products or services to enhance their life experiences or solve problems, and you may have just the perfect solution for them. Think about the game-changing products that you use daily, like bottled water or mobile computers. There was a time when no one believed these two innovative products would become the norm. Evaluating how your talents may bring value to others is a great starting point for you.

When I advise high school and college-ready young adults, one of the discovery questions I ask is what degree are they pursing? Whether their charted course is to obtain four-year or two-year college degree, trade school or some sort of other skill set, this is important to identify. The rationale is there are literally thousands of graduates who have degrees, credentials and/or certifications that do not translate into real world applications. One interesting case study showed the degrees of graduates with majors in leisure studies, fine art or community health had few viable options for employment when they entered the workforce. Many had never asked the basic question, "What am I going to do with this degree and coursework I've spent the last four to five years obtaining?" They quickly found out, which was not articulated to them during their undergrad advisory process, their decision didn't materialize in the marketplace. Properly vet and decide your path of education or acquired skills, and be sure it provides valuable goods and services.

For those of you already happily employed, make the bold decision to expand upon your service at work. Utilize your gifts, maximize your talents, and acquire new skills for promotional opportunities. This will be a great benefit for your family and yourself.

MOVE ASIDE EXCUSES

Many people are experts at rationalizing why they failed at achieving or even starting their pursuits. Excuses build nothing. Excuses tear down any progress towards achieving a goal. Excuses act as a barrier to keep you from even starting.

Excuses are a major kryptonite to success.

"I'm Not Deserving"

Ask yourself, "Who put this thought in my head and when did I buy into this lie?" The idea that you are worthy is critical to achieve whatever you want to become. When you feel as though you do not deserve, you diminish your own self-worth. There is much you bring to the table and can contribute to the world. Decide to adopt an "I am deserving" mindset. Be bold, reflect daily and realize the value you bring.

"I'm Not Smart Enough"

By which metric did you determine that you are not smart? Truth is, everyone is smart at something. It's just a matter of finding where your genius is, as Dr. John Demartini states in *How to Awaken Your Genius*. He emphasizes that once your highest values (daily tasks and actions that require no outside motivation) are identified, you can begin to live your best life. You must be truthful by identifying what moves you, and then move and build on this realization. Decide that you are more than smart enough to achieve what you set out to become.

"It's Too Late"

This is common excuse used by adults, no matter their age. This could not be further from the truth. As long as you have the gift of life, new opportunities can be pursued. The only thing holding you back is your limiting beliefs. Once you are convinced that this is a worthy pursuit that you are passionate about, decide to find a way. Decide the time to start is now, then be bold, defy the odds and make your move.

"I Don't Have the Money"

When you are broke, this excuse can seem like a mountain too high. Don't allow the lack of money to keep you from making moves that will improve the life of your family and yourself. Ideas cost you nothing. That's a good starting point. Certainly, there are pursuits that require capital, but know there are tons of resources and alternatives available. Do the research and expand your mindset to think outside the box. This process will require plenty of work and you have to believe you and your idea, product or service is worth it. When you make the decision that you have enough and that you will find a way, you will find people who believe in your vision who are willing to invest in you.

"What If I Fail?"

The fear of failure is at the top of the list for most people. Every successful person has failed many times over. Inventor Thomas Edison famously said, "I have not failed. I've just found 10,000 ways that won't work." Could you imagine life today without light bulbs? That seems unfathomable. His failures led to one of the most productive careers of all time with nearly 1,100 patents. Seems like a life well served. This is the attitude you want to embody. The "What now?" question is embedded in a decision to press on, especially when the current state of things looks like failure. Now, what are you going to do? Maybe changing course and adjusting, but not giving in to permanent failure. Decide that failure is not an option, then keep working until, like Edison, you find the version that finally works.

The solution to overcoming excuses is to recognize them and identify their origin. Then, make the decision be a "can do" person instead of rationalizing a "can't do" mindset. Overcoming these limiting beliefs is paramount as you push forward in creating a better life and pursuing your goals.

SHARE NOT

You have an idea. You want to change companies. You want to write a book. You want to create a product. You want a promotion. Whatever you want, it is an improvement to your life and will bring you a prosperity and increase. Once this idea takes hold in your mind, you will likely be filled with uncontrollable excitement. That level of enthusiasm is hard to contain, and you may want to share with anyone who will listen. Proceed with caution.

In the Bible, when Jesus Christ's transfigured appearance occurred on the mountain, he told his closest followers: "Tell the vision to no one until the Son of Man is risen." With this, he wanted to ensure that the men who witnessed the miracles he performed would not let anyone know of what was to come (including his suffering, death, and resurrection). The valuable lesson here is to keep your greatest ideas close to home, mainly to yourself.

If it is to be shared, make sure it is with someone for whom you have great respect who can provide you with beneficial counsel. Business partners, investors and mentors would be a few examples of those who could be a part of your plans and vision.

Dreams and vision need a healthy environment to grow. People who love and care for you, may try to talk you out of pursuing your dream if it is big or requires great risk. This happens a lot. Their concern is not about them believing in you, but the love they have for you is a matter of protecting you from disappointment.

Conversely, some friends, family and acquaintances will not support you because of their own disdain or envy. They are uncomfortable when you decide to make a bold move and step outside of the safe box or take your feet off the hamster wheel. Your bold decision to become more and earn more sets you apart from those content with how things are right now.

The bottom line is once the cat is out the bag and your vision leaves your head and comes out of your mouth, detractors will arrive. Though you will encounter them along the way, there's no need to send them an invitation.

EMBRACE YOUR MINISTRY

Whatever path you choose, know that it is yours to embrace. Remember, you are chosen and what you chose has chosen you also. Your goal and pursuit are bigger than you. This is the mindset to embody when taking your ideas into action in the physical world.

What is now visible was once invisible. A thought, idea or flicker in your mind is where it started. When this idea is put into action, a positive result is the conclusion. This result and action will benefit more than you. Whether you consider yourself a religious person or practice faith of any kind, this notion is still relevant. There was a conversation taking place between a mentor and mentee some years ago. The two were talking about a possible new profession path to pursue. The mentor told the pupil to proceed with the new plan as part of his ministry. The pupil said that he was not looking to do work within a church or operate at all in a spiritual capacity. The mentor laughed and briefly explained the concept he introduced.

"The work you are choosing to do is valuable. There-fore, your path, if service is rendered within your works, is your ministry."

The mentor was correct. By definition, to minister is to give service, care, or aid; attend, as to wants or necessities. Notice the wording here. In essence, all paths of work or service are a form of ministry. The barber ministers to his customers while providing grooming, which helps the patrons physically present themselves positively, enhancing their self-image. A teacher provides ministry while educating future generations by empowering students. The landscaper expresses works of ministry while beautifying the yards of customers, by making the neighborhood an inviting place. Even the retail cashier clerk has a quick moment to minister their consumers while purchasing needed products. We are all ministers in our own unique way. There is a longing as humans to connect with others through the works and services. Lean into this knowing and become one who delivers through useful works, deeds, and words in multiple areas of your life.

WHERE ARE YOUR WINS?

Sometimes you have a down moment in life. Or, maybe, you have a lot of them. And as the old adage about tough times states, "when it rains it pours." These moments of distress, whether a death in the family, a major loss in divorce court, one of your kids is flunking in school, or simply being overwhelmed by a job where you are miserable have a piling on effect.

When it seems like the losses are piling up and there seems to be no wins in sight, it is time to dig deeper, be creative and really take a closer look at where in your life things are going in your favor. This begins with an acknowledgement in gratitude, but this for example the focus is more on your skills, expertise, and service.

Let's take a look at my friend Daryl. He and I reconnected after a twenty-year hiatus. In high school, Daryl was a solid student-athlete, a well-liked guy and one who was poised for a great future in whatever profession he chose. But things didn't quite turn out that way.

We met over a cold one to catch up on what was going on in our personal and professional lives. He shared this eye-opening statement.

"Of all my friends, only three of you turned out to be successful. You are one of them and I'm proud of you. Me, I don't know what I have going on. I'm broke, have no car, and have two legal cases pending against me. Right now, I don't have a clue what I want to do with my life. I guess I'm just a failure."

At that time, Daryl didn't have a car or regular employment, and was working odds and ends jobs when he was able to get rides. In addition, he was settling a contentious divorce and was due in court for felony charges in a couple weeks. Now laid off from his most recent job, I could tell his pain was palpable.

However, I knew he was a man of value, but he failed to see it in this low-tide moment. He could not identify where his wins were. He believed there were no solutions to his problems and had nothing to build upon. The conversations turn into an avalanche of self-pity. The storm he was experiencing was real.

I carefully listened and he mentioned that he had mechanic skills, which began a new dialogue.

Daryl: "I was working on cars when I was married, but (through the divorce) she took all my tools."

Me: "That seems like a valuable skill. Why not pursue that again?"

Daryl: "She has all my tools so I can't."

Me: "Do you still have the knowledge to do the work?"

Daryl: "Well, yes. But how can I work on cars without tools?"

Me: "The tools are not the issue. You said that you have little to no value and you just told me that you do. Don't you see that as a win?"

Daryl: "Yeah, I guess I never thought about that."

He also added that he was efficient in HVAC repair, carpentry work and could install any major appliances in residential homes. I told him those trades are essential services that people need, and professions that pay well. He just needed to find the ideal situation to utilize those skills.

Daryl: "Man, I just never thought about it. I've been denied so many times that I'm not sure what to do next."

Over the next few weeks, Daryl and I researched privately-owned HVAC companies, auto repair shops and general contracting opportunities throughout the city. Eventually, he landed a job with a private HVAC business, a paid internship opportunity. This gave him a sense of self-worth, income to address his legal issues and provided him with a sense of normalcy in life. Daryl made a decision to use the knowledge he had and changed his life for the better.

You, too, may be at a place where you don't see a path out, or feeling like the rain you've endured has turned into a flood. When you are able to look beyond the circumstances and into your value, skills, and education, you'll find that the foundation to creating this new life you desire is within reach.

Final Thoughts on Making Decisions with Hjortur Smarason

Make a Decision to Become More

How important has decision making been to your successes?

I have learned that even more harmful than making the wrong decision is making no decision. You can never make the perfect decision so don't wait for things to be perfect or the timing to be exactly right. Just do it. Often you see very fast if it was the right decision or not and then you cancel, change course, or adapt. Success doesn't come to those who wait for it but to those who actively seek it and are willing to make mistakes and fail several times over.

Name a time in your life or professional career when making a decision was used effectively.

I have moved three times between countries, each time to start a new phase in my studies or career. As we have seen with Covid, you can adapt incredibly fast when you are forced to. I can take as an example the summer of 2012. I was unhappy with the political and economic environment in Iceland. I had been a campaign manager for a presidential candidate that stood for change—and we lost. That told me change was not bound to come for the next few years. I had thought about moving abroad but decided in July not to do so. In August, a new opportunity came up and I decided to embrace it full force and three weeks later I had rented out my house, packed everything into a container, found schools for the four kids who were moving with me and moved to a new country. It is amazing what can be accomplished when you put your mind to it and backing out is not an option.

What specific project or accomplishment in particular was making a bold decision most imperative to you?

It doesn't always have to be something big. I once got a request on twitter for a recommendation for a speaker on a certain topic for an international conference. Instead of referring to someone else I saw an opportunity to offer to do it myself. A month later I had started my career as an international speaker with a talk called "Never Waste a Good Crisis," which opened up doors to a number of international consultation projects on the topic. I have now given talks in well over 20 countries on four different continents and run high profile consultation projects on the topic.

How would you advise someone who is down on their luck and has not been decisive in making decisions up to this point?

You don't win the lottery unless you play. It doesn't really matter which numbers you choose, just that you actually do choose some numbers. Your success in life is the same way. You need to be out there, position yourself in the right place at the right time for luck to find you. So do not fear your decision, it is not as important what you decide as it is that you actually do decide. Be out there!

In addition to making decisions, what is another important principle that was used that has been beneficial to your success?

Scenario planning. It is a very important part of any serious decision-making process. It is not enough to look at the resources you have, but also how it can play out in the future, how different stakeholders and external forces can impact the results and most importantly, how each scenario fits your desired end goal. Because you do not necessarily want to choose the easiest or safest way, you want to choose the right way and use all the obstacles you identify in your scenario planning to prepare for them and be better equipped to respond and overcome them once they arise.

Please share some parting words for those who need an added push and words of encouragement to begin pursuing their life goals with a sense of purpose.

What's your story? Each story has a purpose, a back story (your personal experiences) and an end goal. A treasure that you want to find, a puzzle you want to solve. Figure out what your story is and every decision after that becomes so much easier. You just need to match it to your story and see how it moves you closer to your goal and to fulfilling your purpose in life. And believe me, sitting on the couch never made an interesting story. Battling failures, mistakes and obstacles however does, so do not fear your mistakes. They are what helps you grow, learn, and become both stronger and wiser. And even though you see little progress with each step, in five years' time from now when you look back you will realize how far you have become. Now throw off the bowlines, set up sails and go write your story. Bon voyage!

Bio: Hjörtur Smarason is a communications specialist who has advised companies, city councils and national governments on their branding, reputation management and crisis communications strategies. He is now the CEO of Visit Greenland, an organization that is responsible for the promotion and branding of the country and the development of adventure tourism in the World's largest island.

Hjörtur's contact information is hjortur@visitgreenland.com

Chapter 3:

Plan

Def: a method for achieving an end

AFFIRMATION: As I continue to press on with the goals I have in mind, I carefully plan my steps, starting in this moment. My winning blueprint begins here.

Here you are, ready to plan. As you think about the plans you want to make for the goals you've decided upon, you will need both your logic and your intuition. This chapter includes the best practices that I've come across during my own journey. Hopefully when you complete this chapter, you will embody the attitude of platinum rap artists Eric B. and Rakim and have your own master plan. Hopefully, you too will be willing to sweat through the grind it takes to reach your goals.

WRITE STUFF DOWN

After sitting still to reflect on your thoughts and deciding what goals are worth pursuing, it's time to place the pen to pad with planning. The seemingly old-fashioned art of physically writing is still a valuable thing. Yes, using a pen, pad, notebook, or any type of paper. Whether you are journaling, note taking, or compiling your thoughts, the best method of recording is pen and paper. With the increased use of technology, it is usually suggested that your computer or phone be the "go-to" for your notepad (I hear this constantly and am mocked by friends and family over this daily). The truth is with a pen in hand, thoughts are stimulated in a different way. When you present your thoughts through traditional writing, you see the words come to life. The process becomes an energetic one. Detaching from technology for a moment inspires you on a deeper level, allowing you to become one with your thoughts and ideas.

I work with clients in all industries and professions and, as part of our agreement, I supply them with two composition notebooks, similar to the ones used in grade school. The key is to get in the habit of writing down notes, ideas and plans each day.

Commit to this process. This is not plea to abandon the apps and schedules on your phone; however, when it comes to the inception of your ideas, seeing them in your own hand-written words is important. Brainstorming new endeavors begins as a mind dump. When these ideas make their appearance, do not be concerned by order and structure, especially when you first start. You just need to get the ideas out of your head and on to the page. Do not judge your ideas at all during this process. When you've exhausted all of your ideas for a few consecutive days (five days is a good target), let them sit for a day without looking at them or tinkering with them. The next day, return back to your written words that are intensely personal because they are in your own handwriting. Review what you wrote. This allows you to reconnect with your ideas and see what resonates. At this time, you may edit and discard what you feel no longer represents you. You may choose to build on an idea previously written. Remember, do not get too overwhelmed in the editing, or pruning process. Use this exercise to work your ideas to a useful and logical plan or pursuit.

BIG 5 OF PLANNING

Planning is in high demand and big business. Several strategies are available, and for the most part they all have value. Whether a planning practice is simplistic or complex, they all work. The trick is to find and use one that works for you. Here are five steps to get you started in sorting and planning for your next big thing, the Big 5 of Planning: Identify. Justify. Specify. Quantify. Magnify.

Identify Your Goal

What do you want? Whether you are seeking to get promoted at your place of work, launch a business, or write a book, knowing what you want is key. As the saying goes, if you don't know (identify) what you want, how will you ever know if you got it (reached your goal)?

Justify Your Goal

Why do you want to become, have, or do this thing? Remember the discussion about finding your why. Here it is again, and it is the fuel to keep you inspired when the going gets tough.

This is the right question for any strategy for any new endeavor. The energy fueling your pursuits and desires need meaning. The pursuit of your goals, especially a long-term, life-changing goal, requires an investment of time (how long will depend on what you choose) and commitment. During this journey you will face many challenges. When those inevitable setbacks arise, and they will, a clear why accompanied by an evaluation of your values will be the fuel you need to persevere.

Specify Your Goal

Get clear and specific. Vague goals produce vague results. To stack your odds for success, clearly define your goals with as many details as you can imagine during the planning stage. It's not enough to say you want to start a business making $100,000 a year. Be specific, such as stating you want to start an automotive business. From this point, you can get more granular with the details, down to categories within your chosen industry. For example, you may decide you want to start an automotive business that operates on the north side of Chicago and focuses on transmission repair for domestic model cars and trucks. Your imagination now has a concrete idea that is easy to visualize.

Quantify Your Goal

Quantifying your goal means adding numbers, such as time and monetary investment needed to fulfill the goal. This will evolve and be modified over time as societal and market conditions are out of your control. How long will it take? How much capital is needed for its fulfillment? Is this a long-term pursuit or one of the building blocks towards something else? Goals can be identified as short term or long term. A proper timetable and projection of costs (sweat equity and financial investment) is important during the planning process.

Magnify Your Goal

Your human mind is a great gift given to you as means to think, reason, and evaluate, based on your beliefs, values, and life experiences. Due to you being alive for more than five minutes, your mind is conditioned to think with parameters and risk. This is great in that it allows you to make rational decisions based on risk assessments. Conversely, this may also hinder your ability to activate your out-of-box imagination. This is not to imply you are not capable, but your mind may have been trained toward certain safeguards, so your planned goals are "realistic" and practical. This is a great quality that provides you the opportunity to assess risk and how much you may need to stretch to successfully achieve your goals.

The best example of expanding your goals beyond practicality comes courtesy of Grant Cardone and his 10X Rule. The 10X Rule says you should set targets for yourself that are 10 times greater than what you believe you can achieve and, you should take actions that are 10X greater than what you believe are necessary to achieve your goals.

Remember, this is all about mindset, and mindset produces results based on your dominant thought process.

UNCOMMON CHOICE

In 1949, then former president Herbert Hoover wrote these powerful words in *THIS WEEK* Magazine. "In my opinion, we are in danger of developing a cult of the Common Man, which means a cult of mediocrity."

These words still have plenty of relevance. As you begin to chart your path and plans, know they will require far more of you than you initially envisioned. Common is the equivalent of just enough, or as Hoover stated, mediocre. You were created to be someone uncommon endowed with the ability to achieve lofty heights. This is your reward and your responsibility.

Everything you enjoy today was created by uncommon people who acted upon uncommon ideas. The way we travel, by airplanes and cars, began with an uncommon idea. Even the revolution with laptops, smart phones, and access to immediate information via the internet was uncommon.

Settling for anything less than your absolute best is a disservice to yourself and to everyone you come in contact with. So, how do you plan for your uncommon life where you strive to be and become your best?

Start planning to work on yourself each day. Allocate time to acquire skills that bring you closer to achieving your goals. This includes research, study time and learning the uncommon habits and work ethic. Remember why you want this. Dream big, have faith and plan to pursue daily. With this mindset and these actions, you will not be disappointed.

If you have been taught to play it safe or to avoid adversity that seems unfair, adopting a mindset that embraces discomfort in the achievement of a valuable goal will be difficult. Howard Schultz, an American businessman and former CEO of Starbucks Coffee said, "In times of adversity and change, we really discover who we are and what we're made of." In short, goal planning takes a willingness to face uneasiness and struggle. To become an uncommon person requires uncommon dedication to your purpose. Success is not something that you will receive freely, it is earned by first planning for it, then putting your plans into action.

Fictional heroes who engage in bold action also plan and prepare. Take Luke Skywalker in *Star Wars: Episode IV – A New Hope*, who made the quest to Alderaan with Obi-Wan to learn the ways of the force and fulfill his destiny. The same could be said of Katniss Everdeen in the *Hunger Games*, who is trained to survive by her mentor. After taking the red pill, Neo (in the *Matrix)*, who also prepared and trained before his final leap of faith that led him to realize that he is The One, an uncommon man.

As you set your goals and plan for their achievement, be bold and be willing to strive for work and service that sets you apart. Become an Uncommon person willing to do uncommon things to achieve your goals.

READ. WRITE. LISTEN. SPEAK.

During the planning process, communication will be integral in your success. The core concepts – read, write, listen, speak – are key components in working through your pursuits. Ten years ago, I began doing career days at elementary schools in the Houston area. To connect and inspire these youngsters, the lessons they were learning each day were the very same ones I used in my business and profession: read, write, listen, and speak. It matters not what goals or endeavors you choose; these core tenets will always play a factor in planning and building.

Perhaps reading is difficult for you even though it is a required skill. In today's world, this does not prevent you from being able to learn about the world in which your goal sits. Make plans to listen to audio books and podcasts, and find subject-matter experts who are willing to share their knowledge. Maybe writing is difficult for you. As with other skills, practice will make this easier. At the same time, figure out strategies to get better at this skill, whether finding templates for different kinds of documents you may need or taking a class at the community college. If public speaking sounds worse than going to the dentist, make a plan for how to overcome the fear.

Of all these skills, listening is the most difficult because we usually listen to reply rather than listening to understand. This means that we can miss important things in a conversation. As you make plans for your goals, also have a strategy for listening for those tidbits of great information that may be a throw-away comment in a conversation or may lead to a huge and needed revelation.

NO BEST PLANS

You've heard this popular line from Robert Burns' poem *To a Mouse*... "The best-laid plans of mice and men often go awry." No matter how much you plan, conditions will change. In fact, the end result may not look at all like you envisioned. It may even go horribly wrong. Be aware of this and don't be alarmed. Instead, be open to adaptation.

American boxer Mike Tyson famously said, "everyone has a plan 'till they get punched in the mouth." Life and new pursuits have a way of revealing the flaws in whatever plans you thought would work. Embrace as this is the feedback, then be willing to alter your plans so you can press ahead in a new direction. Those who can focus on their end goals, while also making edits along the way, will achieve at a high level.

SEE BIG, SET SMALL

Some of the goals you set are so big that you may wonder, "how and when will I make this happen?" Pursuing lofty goals can lead you to question whether you have what it takes to complete them. If you have failed before or become discouraged at your lack of progress, could it be because you've not set up a system to where you can measure your progress?

A coach I know shared a simple truth, "when you feed a baby, what's the first thing you do? You take the food and cut it up into smaller parts so that they don't choke." This is the same concept to use with goal planning.

As you create a plan for something with multiple components, consciously plan to work in the reverse order of your plan. The "Work in Reverse" principle requires you break your goals into progressively smaller tasks so you can see which ones need to be done first. Take an ordinary weekly goal of exercising four hours. You obviously can't do the whole thing all it once, so you might devote one hour every other day. Then create an exercise plan for those days. You may have a determined a combination of weightlifting and running to best serve you. Each day, you begin with that smallest task and work toward the weekly goal. You plan forward but work in reverse.

This strategy can be used for any undertaking. Declare the end result and devote the time to work it out in smaller, attainable goals is the key. Remember, it's not about simply setting a goal and working on it when it feels convenient.

It's about making the plan to collect small wins and progress along the way that most is important. Along the way, remember to enjoy the journey.

Maybe you are working towards a promotion, learning a new skill, going back to school for a credential or saving money for a worthwhile cause. For any large project, the work in reverse principle can be implemented. In my own life, I have seen again and again how this principle works, which began as a principle experiment that I'll never forget.

When I was blessed to receive my first professional opportunity, I was a year out of college. My salary was $36,000 a year, which was not a large salary, but was the most money I had earned to that point. After years at this startup company, I met my mentor, a man who was an expert on wealth building and investments. He had encouraged me to invest a portion of my earnings, though I was convinced that I had nothing to spare after paying my monthly expenses.

He suggested that I open a saving account and set up automatic deposits into this account.

Mentor: "You need to start saving money. This is important so that you don't find yourself living check to check."

Me: "Okay, but I don't have enough to save at the moment. When I make more, I'll start saving."

Mentor: "Set up automatic payments and begin saving five dollars a month. If the money comes out automatically, you'll never see it and won't miss it. It will be like when taxes are taken out."

Me: "Five bucks. Please, that doesn't seem like it's even worth it."

Mentor: "It's all about creating a new habit and working your way to start saving. It's not about the amount, but the account."

It's not the amount but the account. That last line has remained in my psyche for nearly fifteen years. This idea goes to the heart of "see big, work small." And to this day I still live by this principle when it comes to saving, which has now expanded into larger investments as well. You see, much like the man who sought out more time to health and fitness, I was able to increase my saving from the original five dollar to ten and then doubled to twenty dollars, then hundreds of dollars monthly. This became a required habit to pay my current and future self every time I was compensated.

The principle of "see big, work small" is easy to see with saving money or paying off a debt. With any goal set, a target must be established. Large goals are achieved through the stepping-stone goals that have visible benchmarks for yearly, quarterly, monthly, weekly, and even daily progress. Plan these with as much care and enthusiasm as you have for the big goal. Then apply the Work in Reverse principle so you don't become overwhelmed. Your morale will rise and your interest in the attainment of your goals will shift from dreams to reality.

THINK OUTSIDE THE BOX

Deepak Chopra said, "Instead of thinking outside the box, get rid of the box."

Truth is most new ideas are labeled as stupid, unworkable, or out of the box when they are first thought of. It takes time to gather enough information to give you the energy to begin pursuing it. Consider this, how many ideas were deemed stupid and unrealistic when revealed during the inception stage. Post-It Notes were the result of a failed experiment to create permanent glue. This opposite, non-permanent, removable glue turned out to be worth millions to 3M. In 1956, Wilson Greatbatch "accidently" invented the artificial pacemaker, which was a gamechanger in cardiac medicine.

What would you do without the use of microwave ovens, Super Glue, X-Ray machines and chocolate chip cookies? All were out-of-box inventions. What out-of-box idea are you going to gift to the world? Yours might be a temporary fad like pet rocks or the next life-saving drug like penicillin or a world-changing technology like bio-degradable plastic.

TWO GOALS TO GO

Maybe you have not been very good at planning. Maybe you have had very organized people around you, or maybe you've operated like me for most of your life… simply "making it up along the way," also known as winging it.

Through planning in strategic steps to achieve your goals, there are times when winging it can be beneficial. For anyone who is in some type of major transition: job loss, divorce, death of a family member or eviction, this may be a method that will help you tread water as you mentally unpack all the changes going on in your life.

I found myself in this position a couple of years into my speaking business when my personal life was turned upside down. The family structure that I had built was no longer sustainable, and my wife and I separated. The home I owned was off limits to me, and I became a reluctant nomad making housing arrangements on a weekly, sometimes daily basis. During this period, I was in complete survival mode, and my focus was a day-by-day mindset of self-preservation.

My "monkey mind," took over, which left me feeling unsettled, restless, confused, indecisive and without any control over my life. In that state, planning was impossible and practices that I knew worked, like meditation, seemed beyond me at this time.

During my season of uncertainty, I learned a skill turned out to be a great benefit for me called Two Goals To-Go. This provided me a meaningful process between winging it and long-term planning.

Two Goals To-Go works by simply setting two achievable daily goals, that's it. When I began this practice, I would write them down, think and pray. I told myself that by day's end, I need to complete these two goals or tasks. These goals were simple, direct, and attainable. I was able to complete most of them. This approach netted me solid results, though I felt like I was living on the edge with little to nothing planned each day.

This was my way of making investments into habits. That practice turned one of the most tumultuous years of my life into one of my best. I landed 22 speaking engagements, the result of setting the attainable goal for one day at a time. This led to an opportunity to host a conference and lead a seminar in Africa (Zambia) and work with professionals in Dubai and Abu Dhabi and Pakistan. This was all created at a time of chaos and turmoil, and while I wasn't following a business plan or solid marketing strategy. This began with Two Goals To Go, a step better than the "in case of emergency" option of winging it that can be sustained until you're in a mental state for more detailed planning.

WHO DO YOU KNOW?

As you begin to plan a new undertaking, you will naturally want to become as knowledgeable as you can to put yourself in the best position to succeed. A major aspect of that is realizing you are not going to reach your goal alone (more on this in the SEEK Chapter). You probably already know people who can assist you, whether it's the person who designs websites, knows how to create podcasts, or someone with direct experience in your desired field.

Take An Expert to Lunch

This may be a literal lunch or via one of the many available tools in this social media era.

You will want to seek counsel from someone who has achieved success or has experience in your endeavor. Choose these people carefully, and keep in mind that your purpose is to learn from them, not explain your own plans. Though you may have those light bulb moments for your own plans, this is not the time to disclose them. Instead, find out their strategies for achieving success and avoiding pitfalls.

This expert may be someone you know only as a mentor or a friend whose judgment you trust. Ahead of time, imagine what is most applicable to your business or goal, and plan your questions for this person. Keep the questions to a minimum, which does two important things: it shows your respect for this person's time and allows you to build a follow-on meeting if there is good rapport between you two. Building this type of relationship allows you to have a roadmap of success.

One of the contributors to this book, Dr. Greg Reid, world-renown speaker, author, and filmmaker, offers this advice: make the commitment each day to reach out to two to three people and request a minimal amount of time by posing a single question. As he states, "the most successful people are the most available people." Meaning, successful people like seeing more people become successful. This is expanded upon in the Seek chapter later in this book.

DOES PRACTICE MAKE PEREFCT?

The common idiom of Practice Makes Perfect applies to planning as much as it does to the actual doing. The statement is usually taken as fact. But is this the truth? Legendary coach Vince Lombardi said that "only perfect practice makes perfect." Psychologist Dr. Josh King says deliberately practicing a new behavior has three effects: One, you get better, and getting better increases the odds that you will be successful. Two, you start to replace the old habits with new ones. Making a plan for your success is a habit that takes practice.

Practice is reinforced with techniques that help you to retain what you learn, to the point your key principles, habits, and activities become second nature. One of these is the "3x10 Technique," taught by Dr. Doug Fields, a development neurobiologist from the National Institutes of Health.

It states that if you practice a skill three times with a ten-minute break in between that your mind will have a stronger connection to long-term memory. Understand this is not a one-time exercise. You will want to repeat this action many times, daily to pursue your own level of mastery. This is a great technique in adopting long-term memory on your quest for excellence.

RETIRE ON POSITIVITY

Getting rest, most importantly sleep, is one of the greatest habits you want to adopt. The science on this is undisputed, as sleep is equally as significant as your water intake. Seven to eight hours is the standard (as any doctor would subscribe), though some opt for an hour more or less based on their energy level and effectiveness to function on a daily basis. Do not take the importance of sleep lightly.

In addition to proper sleep, rest helps to put your control center (your mind) at ease. After a long day this is not an easy task, but a necessary one. Speaking from one of the greatest challenges in my own life, finding ways to relax, disconnect and get hours of rest is a job in itself. One of the key factors to addressing this issue is to end how you start on a positive note. One important aspect of rest is that you are providing your subconscious mind (your creative mind) time and space to play. After a good rest, you will not only have more energy, but you will also feel more creative.

Here are a few ways to ensure that you end the day with positive sleep.

Turn it Off

Let's start by what not to do. There are many reasons why the items that dominate your life needs to be turned off when it's time to retire the day. Your phone, cable television, the internet and even your emails need to be shut down, stored away, and turned off. Ending your day trying to catch up will likely trigger emotions that hinder your sleep. All of that, whether the latest on social media or some unfinished task, will be there in the morning. Let it go.

Affirmations

Affirming the thoughts you want to take to sleep with you are just as effective as the ones you say at any other time of the day. Here are a few that you may recite to yourself to close out your day:

I Am Grateful

I Am Love

I Am at Peace

I Choose to Forgive

Any of these statements could spark more thoughts. If this happens, simply take them into short prayer. The key here focusing on thoughts that bring a smile to your face, perhaps recalling a beautiful moment you had during the day. Affirmations as you drift off to sleep plant your mind with the ideas you want to grow.

Keep a Gratitude Journal

Spiritual leaders and the most pragmatic business leaders advise a gratitude journal as an effective way to recognize what you are grateful for. In the Reflect chapter, we introduced the 3G Approach for the morning where you list two things you are grateful for and one goal. To close your day, list all the things that make you feel a sense of gratitude. These can be as simple as what made you smile that day. There can never be too much acknowledgement of gratitude. Using a journal, notepad or even a sticky note can work for this exercise.

Reading

A good book is a great way to close out the night. When reading, there are two key points to make this habit effective. One, choose an actual book with pages you can turn. That's right, a physical book. Remember, you've been viewing screens all day. Physically reading and turning pages is ideal as opposed to an eBook or Kindle. And two, select a book that is interesting to you, though not too mentally intense. The idea here is that if you read a book that has you thinking too deeply you may be prevented from disconnecting and going to sleep.

Meditate/Pray

Ending the day in quiet time, stillness and prayer is always a great option to settle your mind. For many people, this is a ritual that leads to a sense of peace and nearly instant sleep. This, too, can be used in conjunction with some of the other bedtime exercises. This gives you the opportunity to express gratitude and bless those around you, including family, friends, coworkers, employees, clients, community, and country.

Background Music

Peaceful and melodic background noise in the can bring you a calm and soothing feeling before bed. Perhaps create a playlist with your favorite relaxing, peace-inducing music. White noise and nature sounds (rain, trickling streams, ocean surf and other nature sounds) can set a relaxing mood that triggers your mind to rest. Whatever you choose, silence, music, or background noise, bring a feel-good vibe for the end of your day.

Final Thoughts on Planning with Cyrus Webb

Plan and Get to Work

How important has planning been in your successes?

I really believe in some ways it's been the key. It's one thing to have a talent, but if you don't think about the best way to use it and in what form, you'll do what you love, then you'll find yourself doing less. For me over the past seventeen years

I have thought about the endgame, and then I do the work to get there. No way I can do that without a plan.

Name a time in your life or professional career where planning was used effectively.

Definitely it would be the birth of my magazine, *Conversations Magazine*, in 2006. It was a risk for me, but I knew I wanted a way to showcase the interviews from my radio and TV show to a new audience. I looked at what Martha Stewart and Oprah had done with their publications and the people they reached. I knew I couldn't start there, but that was definitely the vein I was looking at when it began. Now, fourteen years later we have over 17,000 subscribers around the world and growing.

What specific project or accomplishment was planning most imperative to you?

For my television show and web-series, *Cyrus Webb Presents*, planning has been essential, especially in 2020 with everything going on. I believe in batch producing so that I'm not rushing. At the beginning of 2020, I was able to travel to Los Angeles and tape an entire season of my show before the country shutdown. That meant I was able to keep fresh content throughout this year without having to resort to repeats.

How would you advise someone who has not planned their actions effectively in their life?

Three things I would say. Look at where you are, think about where you want to go and then start today making the plan to get there. It's really that simple. For me planning has helped me both personally and professionally. It also helps me to celebrate the small gains on the way to the big goal.

In addition to planning, what is another important principle that you use that has been beneficial to your success?

That's simple: remember that your journey is your journey. Don't compare yourself to others. Find those who can motivate you, guide you, but at the end of the day embrace your journey as a unique individual. That will keep you from getting discouraged when you don't see yourself where others are.

Please share some parting words for those who needed an added push and words of encouragement to begin pursuing their life goals with a sense of purpose.

Understand that you are unique and someone in the world needs you. No one can be you. No one can have the impact that you can have. When you embrace that, you'll remember daily why it's important to show up each and every day.

Bio: Cyrus Webb is a radio and television personality, Editor-In-Chief of *Conversations Magazine*, author, Social Media Influencer and Top 300 Amazon.com Reviewer. Since 2003 he has built the Conversations brand into an internationally recognized force that not just shares the stories of others but is making a difference in the way that people see themselves and what is possible. In 2020 Webb has been growing his brand, celebrating seventeen years as the host of Conversations LIVE radio show and fourteen years as leader of *Conversations Magazine*, which is also a top bestseller on Amazon with eleven straight issues reaching the top 200. His new book *WORDS I CHOOSE TO LIVE BY* continues his mission to motivate and inspire others to reach for their goals.

Cyrus Webb's contact information is available at www.cyruswebb.com

Chapter 4:

Act

Def: to do something for a specific purpose or to solve a problem

AFFIRMATION: Today I am committed to taking action on the goals I have set forth. My purposeful actions are what is needed for my goal to become a reality.

GET IT DONE

Whether your tasks are daily, weekly, or monthly, just get it done. Getting it done requires an honest look at the proper time to complete a given task. If you set a time of completion, look carefully at the complexity, as well as the urgency.

Parkinson's Law states that work expands to fill the time available for its completion. Meaning, if you give yourself two weeks to complete an assignment that only requires a day, then the assignment will increase in complexity and will become more challenging to fill a two-week timeframe you gave yourself.

The work smarter strategy overcomes this by breaking large tasks into hours and minutes. Treat these immediate, achievable tasks in the same way you do with goal that is large in scope. Breaking a large goal into smaller, manageable bits will assist you in being more efficient and prevent you from being bogged down. To illustrate let's take a look at how you prepared for a test in high school.

Preparing for a test requires having proficiency in the assigned materials. For example, there are four chapters for a history exam. You have two weeks to prepare. If you spend two hours per day studying, you have twenty-eight hours total or a possible, seven hours devoted for each chapter. This example shows how to allocate your time to the task so you have adequate preparation.

Working with a sense of urgency will help you identify and eliminate time wasters. Just doing it especially applies to the mundane tasks that you may want to save for a later time. Don't. You will save yourself from inefficiency and frustration.

PERSEVERANCE AND PATIENCE

How often have you been told one of these? Hold on. Wait for it. Just a little longer. Be patient. Not quite yet. Be aware that having patience and waiting for something to happen are not the same thing though the ideas seem related.

Here's a point to consider: How long are you willing to wait for your goals to be achieved?

The old school principle rings true: the best things come to those who wait. However, waiting is not a passive sitting around until things happen, but rather continuing to work toward goals step-by-step. In other words, cultivate patience while you diligently work toward the achievement of your goals. It's true that sometimes it may take seven years to become "an overnight success" or "10,000 tries" before the light bulb illuminates. Along the way, you continue to work toward your goal, taking care of the things that need to be done at each step. Patience is the process of effort and time working together to achieve a result.

Perseverance is the continued effort to do or achieve something especially in the face of difficulties, failure, or opposition. It's all in the doing towards goal attainment. To ensure this level of focus, create habits that reinforce the attainment of the goal no matter how challenging or boring today's tasks are. One of these habits is your commitment of time each day to work on your project, which includes some tasks you find tiresome and some you love doing. They all require your effort over time (patience) and your diligent focus (perseverance) to meet your bigger goals.

To see this at work, watch a baby learning to walk. He doesn't just stand up and immediately run. He will use a coffee table as a brace to pull himself up, and when he takes those first steps, he will fall again and again, but if he keeps at it with time and effort (patience) and diligent focus (perseverance) until he can walk, then run. Entrepreneur Richard Branson defeated the failure of Virgin Records by launching Virgin Radio that same year, which led him to his second record label, V2, three years later.

Recognize it will take time for your goals to materialize. Keep in mind these two Ps (patience and perseverance) act as partners as you continue to work. Consistently, think about your dreams and goals firmly grounded in your strong belief that your undertaking will unfold in ways that surprise you at the appropriate time.

BE A BUILDER

Every day it is imperative to have a constructive mindset to build and create.

In the last chapter, you were provided tools to plan. Now, act to implement those plans. Hopefully when you awaken, you have goals and tasks for the day laid out. Your earnest attention is required for you to fulfill your daily tasks. If you have no clear plan, then your actions will likely be off track. If this has happened to you, maybe you need to reevaluate your plan. Here are a few things to consider.

Never Quit

"Never, never, never quit." At the time Winston Churchill made this simple statement during WW II, Great Britain was under the threat of invasion by Hitler's Third Reich. The successful resistance by the British was no sure thing. "Never quit" gets right to the point. Determination and a concentrated hustle are needed to be an effective builder. When the outcome is most in doubt, double down on your commitment to see your endeavor through to the end. When an intense grind and endurance is required, dig deep for the motivation to keep going by focusing on the end, not on the current, perhaps difficult things that need to be done.

Adapt in Real Time

This goal of yours that has become a burning desire requires both single-minded focus and your ability to adapt to changing conditions, such as the pandemic of 2020 and 2021 that changed how everyone works and lives. When you are presented with new obstacles or opportunities, be willing to adapt. Check in with your trusted advisors whose insights will be invaluable to you. Be curious and do your research before jumping ship or hopping on a new one. Be open to revising your plans. Be willing to take a leap of faith to meet changing conditions while at the same time keeping your end goal in mind.

Chart Your Progress

As you press forward with your goals, be sure to check your results on a daily, monthly, and quarterly basis. Day by day, you may not think you're making much progress, but when you look at your advancements over a month or several months, you will see you are making headway. Goals are met one small step at a time, and so your greatest feedback comes by measuring your progress frequently. At the end of each day, write down the next steps needed to reach your goal. This pragmatic habit allows you to see your progress over time, keeps you accountable, and also reminds you with why you fell in love with this endeavor. This habit keeps you operating at a high level.

HAVE A PURPOSE ON PURPOSE

Remember the "why" established in the DECIDE chapter? The why is the source of your inspiration for the goal you are working to achieve. This why is the purpose for your goal and so it needs to be on purpose (no pun intended).

Being on purpose is a song worth putting on repeat. As you take action on the tasks before you, remember they are indeed bigger than you. Keeping your why in mind empowers and inspires you to move forward toward your goal. The best part is your example will inspire others who may not yet have found the passion and drive that you embody. Your will unintentionally liberate others by the example set by your life energy, dedication to your craft and your faith. The fuel for being on purpose with your purpose is the "why." How will you know that you embracing your purpose? You arise early, stay late and completely lose track of time as you work to achieve your goal.

Your purpose is a gift. Unwrap it and share so that others may do likewise.

BE A HERO

The hero of any story is the person who acts, who make things happen, and who rises to the occasion to overcome adversity and succeed. You may be thinking, am I a hero? The answer is "Absolutely yes." You are the hero of your own story, and if you envision the achievement of your goal as a hero's journey, you are better able to face the ups and downs along the way.

Joseph Campbell spent decades studying literature, mythology, and world religions that resulted in his theory of the hero's journey, *The Hero with a Thousand Faces* (1949). For those of us who love movies, the hero's journey is a familiar one from the call to some sort of adventure to defeating a villain, learning valuable life lessons, and achieving the ultimate rewards of success.

Your own hero's journey begins where you are right now. Like all heroes, something within you wants to be and become more. You went through a process of reflection (Chapter 1), decided on a course of action based on your big "why," (Chapter 2), made a plan (Chapter 3), and now you're ready to act to fulfill the goals you strive for. Like all heroes, you are journeying a road from ordinary to extraordinary.

Every sensible hero will have doubts, maybe to the point of refusing the call because the endeavor seems too big, too scary, or too difficult. Your desire to pursue this big goal may be renewed after conversations with your mentor or a yearning to become more and accomplish more than you ever had before. The desire may also come to you spiritually as a dream. And so, you take the leap.

New challenges are thrust upon you, and you receive the guidance needed to press forward through obstacles or apparent failure. Along the way, you will acquire the skills, contacts, and knowledge needed to succeed. However, at some point, you will likely have that dark night of the soul when failure seems at hand. Going back is not an option, so you press forward with a "never quit" mindset, and you gain more strength, skill and confidence with every challenge faced. You unlock your determination and discipline as you tap into your unrealized potential.

When you achieve your goal, you will likely realize it has yielded rewards beyond what you imagined in the beginning. Your compensation arrives in the form of wisdom, fortitude, and a better understanding of what it takes to succeed. With this knowledge and discovery, you are prepared for the next journey. Your development has come full circle where your new ordinary world is grander than it was when you first thought of the goal.

As you work toward your goals, you will discover you have within yourself the heroic qualities you admire, among them courage, determination, loyalty, and love, heroic qualities inherent in everyone, including you.

MAKE TIME COUNT

As shared in the "Eyes on Your Paper" in the Reflect chapter, your focus should always be centered on your own process. A primary factor is to value time. Planning and prioritizing how to spend time is a trait of every successful person and is key to your goal achievement.

As you plan your schedule, take a close look at your tasks with these two questions. Is this task important to the achievement of my goal? Is this task urgent? Items that are not urgent and not important to the achievement of your goal may include doing a favor for a friend, may be something you can delegate, or may be total time wasters. Look closely at these so you can choose whether this is where you should be spending your time. Tasks that are both urgent and important are similar to putting a bucket under a leaky pipe to keep from flooding a room, but may not address the real problem, like shutting off the water so the leak can be repaired. As you plan your time, you want to work as much as possible on tasks that are important and immediate, but not yet urgent. In this way, you can work effectively without being stressed out, where you are focused on taking care of today's stuff today.

Identify two or three of the most important tasks on your list, which become your priority items for the day. The Pareto principle, known as the 80/20 Rule, is one strategy for prioritizing your tasks. The rule states twenty percent of your list will produce eighty percent of the results you will achieve for the day.

The combination of planning and prioritizing will ensure you act with focus to ensure your time and effort result in the maximum output in your workday.

OWN THE PROBLEM, NOT THE FAULT

Sometimes you may be faced with an issue that you did not cause. One such instance that happened with me was the discovery that my yard was littered with trash, due to stray dogs rummaging through the neighbor's trash bags adjacent to my property. Since my family's trash was secure inside metal bins, the problem was not the result of my neglect, so it was not my fault. However, since the trash was in my yard, cleaning it up was my problem and my responsibility. This type of thing happens to all of us, and the trick is to accurately define the problem, create solutions and avoid blame.

Here is a process to work through any challenge before you.

First, identify the problem. There can be no solutions until this is determined. To illustrate, after years of working menial jobs with low earnings, you may decide that you want to become a physical therapist. Second, you explore solutions by researching schools that offer the instruction you need, the requirements for your admittance, and the cost. Third, you implement an action plan by meeting with a school counselor to obtain financial aid and register for the required prerequisite classes.

So, what was learned here?

There are problems and there are solutions. You want to embrace both, squarely looking at the problems, but being focused on the steps to achieve a solution. It is worth remembering that solutions are never found by blaming or remaining stuck inside the problem, but instead by clearly understanding it so you can see its possible solutions.

NO FAIRY TALE LIFE

Frederick Douglas said, "without struggle, there is no progress."

There is no pot of gold, magic genie or Thanos snap that will prevent adversity. Abraham Lincoln faced failure in the military, law, business and even politics before becoming one of America's greatest presidents. In nature, the caterpillar suffers an apparent death before its metamorphosis into a butterfly.

Struggle creates the on-the-job-of-life education you need to succeed. It gives you the insight to press on and create. Remember, you overcame most of the issues you've faced, even though some are still a work in progress.

One notable example is actor Jim Carrey who overcame poverty and homelessness during his teen years. At fifteen, he dropped out of school and moved to Los Angeles to launch his acting career. Along the way, he struggled through numerous adversities for many years before his first successful films. He famously wrote himself a check post-dated ten years for $10,000,000, which was the amount of his first royalty check after the movie *Dumb and Dumber* was released. His example illustrates that effort is required on a sustained basis before getting to that great biography of achievement you want to claim as your own.

BE COMFORTABLY UNCOMFORTABLE

Ralph Waldo Emerson said, "Always do what you are afraid to do."

If you are anything like me, you figure out what you're already good at and feel confident doing. Being recognized as competent is reassuring and comforting, and it's tempting to stay in this place. As you work toward the achievement of your goal, you will encounter instances where your skills and knowledge fall short. You are then faced with the choice to shrink your idea so you stay within your comfort zone, or you can take that scary leap into the unknown. Of course, the scary leap is where the potential to succeed is. To help you feel more in control, become a continual learner where you research everything you can about your endeavor, including pitfalls that may never happen. Some of those pitfalls may be scary, such as testing your physical limits or risking your life savings. Specifically identify those fears, then develop a detailed plan for what you can do in the face of any obstacle you encounter.

Remember your values that are part of your goals, which will keep you centered about why they are worthy of your time and attention during the hard times. And finally, redefine failure as learning opportunities. No setback is a permanent failure unless you label it as such; instead, setbacks are often the springboard for the next step of the journey toward the achievement of your goals.

I recall a time when my father helped me step out my comfort zone by having me race with eighth-grade track runners when I was only in sixth grade. At that time, I was intimidated and embarrassed. The reward came when I earned a spot on the high school varsity track team as a freshman. By the time I left high school, I had broken five school records. I learned that improvement comes by pushing past what you believe is possible.

Become comfortable being uncomfortable sounds like an oxymoron, but it is the fuel needed for your success. Pressure tests your mental faculties, preparing yourself for the greater moments ahead. Lean in and embrace the pain in your higher pursuits. Trust and know that a beautiful story will emerge in your quest for your goals.

BE BUSY DOING IT

Spiritual leader Michael Bernard Beckwith said, "Don't tell me what can't be done, I'm too busy doing it."

These words should resonate with you while pursuing your goals. Your plans are decided, written and you are ready to make moves. Here is something to keep in mind, distractions along the way are inevitable. These roadblocks come in many forms, such as negativity from people, unexpected challenges, or a lack of focus. Here are a few ways to remain calm and steadfast in your pursuits.

If your goal is to write a book, set an assigned time every day to do that on a regular schedule. Commit to producing a specific number of new words every day. If your goal is to produce 500 new words every day, and if a typical chapter of a book has 5,000 words, it will take you ten days to produce that material. The pitfall to committing to time instead of outcome is that you may be tempted to spend your time (as it relates to this example) rewriting instead of writing something new. Having a production goal will help you see that you are making forward progress.

So, get busy working towards a definite end. Then get some rest and start the cycle again.

EMBRACE THE F WORD(S)

No… not that F word. Instead, make these empowering words for you while pursuing your goals and working towards positive life changes.

Fair

Truth is, the game of life is not fair, and never will be. You will be faced with making choices that come at the expense of others, thus negating true fairness. At that point in time, it becomes a tradeoff. In baseball, a Fielder's Choice is a great example, by choosing to throw out a player on the field instead of the batter. Life will present you with unique challenges, and you will need to assess the risks. When you make the just and loving choice, that is as close to fair as you can be.

Free

Free, in terms of value, is the idea that something comes to you at no cost. This couldn't be further from the truth. You are likely familiar with the saying, "There is no free lunch." Everything has a cost, which may be hidden. If you have a scholarship for college, a hidden cost is the need to maintain a specific GPA. The hidden cost for that is the time you spend studying instead of earning money at a job. Most of the time, these hidden costs are related to your time. So, you need to see your time as your most valuable asset that you guard in the same way you would guard your wallet.

Feelings

Feelings are an informational resource that let you know how committed and connected to something you are. Feelings are a built-in feedback mechanism that gauge your commitment about something. These feelings can be guides that help you gauge the best way to make consequential decisions. Your mind is responsible for rational thoughts, while feelings come from the heart. But they must also be weighed with rational judgment. Sometimes, these are easy. Your feeling to be accepted by your friend who wants to let him drive after a couple of drinks has to be weighed with the rational thought of this being a bad choice. Sometimes, these are harder, such as the need to lay off an employee to make payroll. Choose wisely when selecting what drives your decisions.

Failure

In pursuit of your goal, you will face many setbacks that you may be tempted to label as failure. The Success Magazine's article, *6 Mindset Principles of Successful People,* identifies failure as nothing more than feedback needed to find out why something didn't work. Rename these "failures" as setbacks, then use them as guides of experience and wisdom for the next attempt.

Facts

Facts are information. Entrepreneur Mark Cuban quite rightly asserts that "information is power, especially when your competitors ignore the same information." The challenge is ensuring your information comes from reliable, credible sources so you are in the best position to make decisions that drive you toward achieving your goals. As you research how to best pursue your goals, follow verifiable facts first and then opinions and theories from your trusted advisors. For example, it's a verifiable fact that about half of all businesses fail within the first five years. But the fact does not address the specifics about your business or your likely success. Your own research will find information about your market, capital requirements, competition, and so on, so your analysis, puts you in the best position possible for success, which may require you go against what seems rational.

INVEST IN YOURSELF

You are probably aware of the saying, "you cannot pour from an empty cup." If you remember back to times when you pursued a big goal, you probably also remember that you were mentally and physically taxed. To maintain your enthusiasm and your energy, you must invest in yourself. Investing in yourself needs to be at the personal level so you are physically, emotionally, and spiritually fit. And, investing in yourself also needs to be at the professional level so you are gaining the skills and knowledge you need to fulfill your goals

At the personal level, invest in yourself by attending to your physical well-being. This might be going to the gym or having an accountability partner who you work out with. Invest in your emotional health by spending time with your loved ones and doing activities that give you pleasure. Invest in your spiritual health by attending to your spiritual practices, whether attending church services or joining a prayer group.

Invest in yourself professionally by taking classes and joining organizations that benefit your business and your growth. For instance, if you need better public speaking skills, join a group like Toastmasters so you have a venue to practice. Other investments in yourself are things like taking classes at your local adult Ed organizations or community college in marketing or accounting or business law that may be directly applicable to your business. Invest in yourself by attending conferences in your industry or by hiring a coach to help you with your areas in need of improvement. Invest in yourself by teaching or mentoring others with what you most want to learn.

Your investment in yourself helps you to maintain enthusiasm over the long haul because you will be learning and associating with people who lift you up.

BECOME VALUE, CREATE VALUE.

These are simple statements, yet not simple to execute. The mission as you pursue your goals is to increase your value;

however, before you can increase your value you must discover your current value.

When I first got into the business of college football recruiting, my break into the profession came because of my journalism skills and my affinity for college football. For years, I hung around camps and showcases hoping to find someone to help me break into this profession. Once I did, I grinded for two years earning a meager stipend. Over the next seven years, I had worked my way into a full-time salary as my secondary job. Along the way, I believed in my own value while at the same time doing my best to create value for the organizations I worked for.

The key is to have courage to travel into the unknown and altering your path (I transitioned from print journalism to online sports blogging) into a new arena. Be willing to learn and grow from new experiences.

To achieve this, take an objective look into your value. This can be challenging and may require feedback from professionals within your circle. Value is measured by the number of useful skills you bring to an organization. Assess, then write down all your skills. This clear idea will help you see how you can add value to what you do, making yourself of greater value and to add value to the organization.

SUCCESS IS ACTION

Success leaves clues. When you pay attention and research the mindset and actions of those who have blazed this trail before you, you see a roadmap as you begin your own journey. One of <u>the</u> trailblazers who studied success habits is Napoleon Hill whose book *Think and Grow Rich* (first published in 1937) continues to spark men and women who follow his principles for success.

While mindset is the starting point of everything achieved in life, the actions that follow with successful people are consistent. It's a relentless discipline that separates haves from the have nots. So, what is it that successful people do that others do not? Here are some actions, which require no money, talent, intellect, or special skills. All that is required is a readiness and effort on a daily basis.

7 Actions of Successful People

Consistent Reading

Successful people read consistently, each day, enhancing their skills, researching the latest trends in their industry, or learning new strategies.

Alone/Quiet Time

Whether at the start or close of day, successful people find a moment to sit still and think. It may be to organize their thoughts, or to simply take a moment to unwind. This brings a level of calm and restoration to a day otherwise scheduled to the brim with meetings and agenda items. Alone time is a key factor for high achievers to max out their awakened working hours.

Exercise

Keeping your body in great physical condition is paramount. Exercise helps your mental state of mind as well. Nearly every person who is successful in any industry has an exercise routine of some kind. Fitness helps with blood flow, generates feel-good endorphins, increases stamina, and overall vitality. In addition to exercise, a well-balanced nutritional routine gives your body the fuel it needs for an overall healthy state of being.

Time is Valuable

Time is one of your most valuable resources because it can never be regained or replaced. Remember the discussion about spending your time on the important and immediate? Successful people are good at identifying what needs to be done now and focusing their time and attention on the most important of those items. Wasted time becomes wasted opportunities, and wasted opportunities may not come around again.

Circle of Success

Successful people hang out with success people. Remember, it's a positive mindset at the center of all of this. As the great entrepreneur John Rohn said, "You're the average of the five people you spend most of your time with." This is a powerful statement. The people you spend time with correlates to your success level in most instances because your mindset vibrates at the same level as those who operate on your level.

When surrounding yourself with others pursuing big goals, you have the opportunity to learn from them and receive the halo effect of their energy, and vice versa. Successful people enjoy being around success because the energy is infectious, leading to a greater success for all involved.

Relentless Pursuit

Successful people have a mindset to keep on going no matter how challenging or big the obstacles. Quitting is not an option for relentless people. Once they set their minds on an objective, they constantly, purposefully, intentionally keep on going no matter what. They learn and they adapt, knowing that luck is really preparation and relentless pursuit. The difference between a successful person and the one who is not is simple: the successful person didn't quit.

Final Thoughts on Taking Action with Christopher Alan Zook

Take Purposeful Action

How important has taking action been to your overall successes?
Without action, there is no success. Only by taking action, with a dedicated purpose, can success be achieved. This is true in virtually every aspect of life. Whether it be in business, sports, or even as a parent, it is hard to make an impact if we do not accomplish what we believe to be important. Everything I have achieved in life would not have occurred if I had not taken focused steps towards a defined purpose.

Name a time in your life or professional career where taking action was most effective.

When my wife, Lisa, and I set a goal to start the firm, we prayed God would give us a timeframe as to when this should happen. For several years, we both felt August 2001 was that date. When July 2001 rolled around, we began to question if that was the right timing for us. Even though, for three years, we felt God leading us to open in August, we debated if we should postpone. "Just for a month," we both said. "What could that hurt?" As the end of July approached, we came to understand that it was fear holding us back, and we knew fear was not a reason to delay. Every time we asked God, "Are we ready? Are you sure it is now," it was as though we could feel a physical push on our backs with a loud voice in our head yelling, "GO!" We stuck with our original date and launched the firm on August 16, 2001. Let that date sink in. "What could one month hurt?" One month later would have been September 16, 2001, five days after 9/11. I still get shivers when I think about this. I do not believe the firm would exist today if we had given into fear. When feeling led, with a clear purpose, do not wait and do not delay. Take action with confidence.

What specific project or accomplishment in particular was taking action most imperative to you and those whom you lead?

In 2013 our business was doing well, but we had so much more potential. The team went through significant strategic planning and determined we had the ability to do what no one else in the industry dared. This action would align our personal interests with the interests of our investors. We restructured the business in a manner that allowed our firm to be paid, almost exclusively, only when our investors made money. The willingness to set ourselves apart from our competition has led to the business growing by more than 600% in the last six years.

How would you advise someone who maybe has been hesitant in taking actions to pursue their goals?

My wife and I like to use the "rocking chair test." This simple exercise will help you overcome most of the hesitancy that can get in the way of taking action to achieve goals. Envision yourself in the last years of your life. You are sitting on a porch, in a rocking chair, looking back over the things you have accomplished and the things you let slip by. Whatever you are contemplating, ask yourself, "At the end of my life, if I do not try to achieve this goal, will I regret that decision?" If the answer is yes, then you need to move forward with your dream. Although no one likes to fail, it is part of life, and we grow from these experiences. But regret? That is a different emotion. Not moving forward, not taking the risk, to achieve a dream, leaves a bitter taste in our mouths that never seems to leave. Success or failure? I can live with this. Regret? I do not want any part of it.

In addition to taking action, what is another important principle that you use that has been beneficial to your success?

If you do not know where you are going, any road will take you there. If you love what you do, you never work a day in your life. These are common phrases, but so true. Without a roadmap, your actions, although well intentioned, may take you far from your intended purpose. But taking action towards a clearly defined goal, a goal that leads to a compelling purpose, is where fulfillment comes from.

Find your purpose. Figure out your passion. Then create a clearly defined path to accomplish the steps that are needed to make your purpose a reality. Once those steps are clear, take action, and you will be fulfilled.

Please share some parting words for those who need an added push and words of encouragement to begin pursuing their life goals with a sense of purpose.

History will not measure us by our failures, but it will hold us accountable for not trying. If we take time to define our purpose, have a strong reason why we want to achieve that purpose, create a defined path with measurable goals, and then take action, we will succeed. Only then will history celebrate our success and the impact we made on this world. Do not wait! Do not delay! Do not sit in your rocking chair and regret not becoming what God created you to be. You were made for a purpose. Find it!

Bio: Christopher Zook is the Founder, Chairman, and Chief Investment Officer of CAZ Investments. With nearly thirty years of experience investing in both traditional and alternative asset classes, he is a regular contributor to major media outlets. Christopher is actively involved in public policy and frequently serves as a resource to state and local officials.

A graduate of Texas Tech University, he is active in his church serving as a deacon, teacher, and on the financial committee for Second Baptist. Christopher has also held leadership positions on numerous charitable boards, both locally and nationally. He is a proud father to Christopher, Jr., and daughter-in-law, Cecelia Schmidt Zook, and husband to his high school sweetheart, Lisa.

Christopher Zook's contact information is available on www.cazinvestments.com

Chapter 5:

Seek

Def: to search for something or to discover something

"He that won't be counseled can't be helped."
–Benjamin Franklin

AFFIRMATION: As I work to attain my goals, I accept wisdom and help from supportive people, and I set my intention to provide the same for others.

Ou your journey to becoming the best version of yourself, two things will be true at the same time. You will be pulling others up as you grow and achieve. At the same time, others will be pulling you up as they grow and achieve. One of the greatest recognitions of becoming successful is that interdependence is a key ingredient. Dependence means you need help. Independence means you can operate on your own. Interdependence means you can do it on your own, but you recognize and appreciate that other people bring wisdom, strengths, and insight that you would not have had without them. Working together is a winning combination. To achieve your greatest levels of success, you need others.

YOU NEED AA

Almost everyone needs an Accountability Ally (AA), who helps hold you accountable to your own high standards. Your AA might be a trusted friend or may be someone you hire, such as a life or performance coach. One of the reasons an AA works for you to stay motivated and meet your goals is because you've made a commitment to someone else. It's true that the day-to-day operations of working your goals must be done by you. It's also true that no one reaches high levels of success alone, no one.

When you find yourself at a crossroads moment, your AA can provide fresh insights to your challenges. Think about those moments when you've hit a wall, tapped out and feeling a bit overwhelmed, your Accountability Ally could help get you back on track. So, who should be your AA?

Seek someone who is knowledgeable in areas where you are challenged, someone who has a positive attitude, and someone willing to be stern and direct when you need your feet held to the fire. Your best AA is likely a person with whom you've had prior connection, good rapport, and mutual respect. This is someone who will deliver needed critique without hesitation and with good intent to help you advance on your goals and plans.

Since you are giving a potential AA the power to influence how you think and how you approach your goals, choose carefully. Think about what you realistically need to hold yourself accountable, then set up the terms and conditions with the person you choose to be your AA.

For me, I have three with who I connect with on a quarterly basis. They include a speaking coach and mental health psychologist, a former CFO and minister, and an international business consultant. These people have different strengths and perspectives that enrich me. They help me sift through challenges and assist me in securing new and profitable opportunities.

Keep in mind that no one gets to a high level of success alone. It takes many trusted people along the way, and you are not the exception. Seek out those trusted and tough individuals who want to help you on your journey. You will be better for it.

SHARE YOUR WHINE

You will have moments from time to time that set you off to the point you may want to publicly post your grievance on your favorite social media platform. In a word, "Don't!" This could bring a level of unwanted attention to you. Instead, talk to a trusted whining partner. It's this person's job to listen while you vent, then offer you suggestions if you ask for them. Sometimes the mere act of venting your frustration will help you see the solution.

Ensure your whining partner is a trusted person who will not turn your meltdown into a pity party where you feel more victimized or out of control. This person's role is to hear you out, calm your anxieties, and help you move toward a resolution.

I remember years ago I called on one of my mentors while preparing for an upcoming event. The agreement was already decided, but the organization changed the terms less than a week before the event. I was livid and called upon this mentor. He listened to my rant and because of the trusted relationship we have, and I was willing to listen when he asked,

"Are you going to do the event or not? If you are not, call them and say, no thank you. If you still want to do it under the new terms, then let's come up with some solutions."

One more point: a whining partner is not to become a whining committee. Having multiple people involved will invite more opinions, leading to more stress. Choose that one trusted person for this role so you have the positive guidance you need when your mind is scattered.

CHECK YOUR ATTITUDE

What kind of people do you like to be around? I bet it is those with a positive mental attitude. Whether people are drawn to you or steer clear of you, your attitude is probably the reason and is reflected in your behavior and the way you carry yourself. You know whether you're eager to meet your day and cheerful about working on the tasks before you or dreading them. Generally, your attitude is a habit. Like all habits, developing a positive mental attitude requires daily work.

Gratitude work, meditation, affirmations, and conversations with people all help you develop a positive mental attitude. It's an ongoing practice that will always produce solid results for yourself and those around you.

Having a positive mental attitude does not mean you deny your feelings when you feel down. Honestly assess why you feel down, and keep digging until you get to the bottom, asking why at each step. For instance, if you feel disappointed or frustrated or angry about something, ask yourself why. Then ask why again and wait for whatever answer comes up. Repeat this until there are no more why's to be revealed. At that point, you're ready to put your attention on what you do want with a positive mental attitude.

Seeking strategies to develop a positive mental attitude is of utmost importance. Here is a daily exercise to use that can put you in a better position to positively work through your daily challenges.

1. Start your day with the intention of keeping positive thoughts…ALL day

2. To measure this, keep track with an index card.

3. On one side, write the word "Challenge" and on the other side "Solution"

4. Throughout the day, for every time you gripe, complain, or speak negation to or about another person, make a single mark on the "Challenge" side of the card (Be honest).

5. On the "Solution" side, list three healthy alternatives to the harmful statements made.

At the end of the day, perform these steps and make your solutions a priority until they become ingrained habits. You may ask what you do if the negation carries over day-to-day, despite your counter positive statement. Negation is mostly masked by fear, whether it's anger, inadequacy, regret, guilt, or frustration. This requires a deeper conversation with yourself.

For example, you are working on a business plan and become frustrated while organizing your core tenets for the business. Is the frustration based on the organizing of the business plan, or are you unclear the structure of the business? Identifying the source of negation is key, and likely a great time to call your mentor or coach for assistance, which is why you hired them.

HAVE YOU HAD YOUR MOMENT?

Remember a time in your life when you faced a major decision, one that forced you to reevaluate or change course? How did you feel when that moment occurred?

For many people, the moment they decide to make a major change comes with an "I've had it. No more!" moment that may have been building for a long time. Such a moment must become unbearable. This trigger might be a crushing debt, a family break up, bad news from a doctor, a job loss, or some other significant emotional experience. This moment may not be immediately life threatening, but it probably feels that way.

Two dominant factors come together. The decision to make a change and a strategy to implement that change that includes seeking the right people and right information to be successful. Such a moment came for me in a dressing room where I was trying on clothes to fit my out-of-shape and overweight self.

For most of my life, I had been a fine-tuned athlete, who played three sports in high school and had a short stint with college football. After my college football career ended prematurely because of an injury, I went to work, ate too much, and stopped exercising. One of my jobs was at local sports bar where I worked as a waiter and bartender. I was living the life, filled with alcohol and fast food. I totally let go of my discipline to eat well and be physically fit. My weight ballooned to 240 pounds, far cry from the 185 pounds with seven percent body fat I had when I stopped playing football.

Then one day I had had enough. My critical moment of clarity came inside a Banana Republic dressing room where the clothes that fit were many sizes bigger than I had ever worn. I had big plans, and none of those fit with the out-of-shape overweight man I saw in the mirror. I remember saying,

"Enough. I cannot go on living like this. I don't even recognize who I am anymore."

That was the first step, that moment of clarity. My second step was to seek out people and strategies to help me get back in shape. My mentor guided me through this process, which was a new challenge for me since I had never experienced excessive weight gain. He explained the science behind eating nutritious foods and having an exercise routine. That night, I began my weight loss journey, which included purging high-fat, high calorie snack foods from my pantry, and replacing those with healthy, lower-calorie choices of vegetables, turkey, and fruits. Since I was determined to succeed, I logged my meals and calories. Since my mentor was my Accountability Ally (AA), I reported everything daily.

On rare occasions, when I went over my intake target, we identified where I had gone off track so I could recommit to doing better. I looked forward to my time in the gym as I reclaimed exercising regularly. Slow and steady, the weight started coming off. I increased the intensity of my routines, and I especially loved the indoor cycling I participated in two to three times a week. My weight began falling off to the tune of two to three pounds a week, and within five and a half months, I had lost forty-six pounds and my waistline shrank from forty to thirty-four inches. The progress boosted my confidence and motivated me to do even more.

I started lifting weights and working with a boot camp. More weight came off, and my body was starting to look and feel as it had during my football days. In total, I lost sixty-eight pounds and I felt and looked like a new person. Along the way, I committed to my new habits that continue today. This also led to new opportunities, and I now teach cycling class as a certified instructor in North Houston. All of this emerged from that "I've had it" moment in a dressing room.

The point of my story is that once you have decided upon a course of action, you need a strategy for success and people to help you succeed. When you provide energy and are making gains, they match your energy in the service they provide to you. Successful people want to see others succeed. Get your ego out of the way and seek what you need to create the life you desire and deserve.

SEEK G.O.D.

You may have called upon the vast knowledge of Siri or Alexa as you seek all kinds of information. Another limitless "database" is available to you and has the advantage of not requiring an internet connection: Good On Demand (GOD). GOD is the spiritual energy force that lives in everyone. This energy is without form, and is a pure, unlimited power. It may be used at any time and is always present. When you have the recognition of this energy, you are positioning yourself to find the people you need to help you achieve your goals. This principle is at work whether you are religious or not and whether you regularly attend a church or not.

This power is always available. It has no limits. You may call on this divine wisdom anytime, but you may especially be aware of it while in your quiet time, be it prayer or meditation. Unlike the smart devices you carry around, GOD has no limitations within its databases. Just as your word has power when you tell Alexa to change TV stations or play a favorite podcast, your word with GOD also has power when you positively state what you want. Your personal relationship with GOD is ongoing, unlimited and is always accessible.

If you cannot imagine where to begin, follow the example of a master teacher, Jesus, who advised,

"Ask, and it will be given to you; seek, and you will find; knock, and it will be opened to you."

Go now and ask for what you need to fulfill that which you seek. Be patient, but also continue working as the answers will come to you in due time and in the right season.

BE BOLD LIKE RJ

Big things come in small packages. As the old quote states, "it's not the size of the dog in the fight, it's the size of the fight in the dog."

Both are famous quotes and set the stage for this story. Here is RJ, a young man who is small in stature, but big in heart. A guy who led the charge and changed the culture of a football team by seeking what they needed to win.

In a small, rural town outside the Houston area, RJ was a member of a football team that was on a nineteen-game losing streak, with its coach searching for answers. The coach and I met while attending a conference. After our talk, he agreed to purchase ten copies of my then newly released book, *Awaken the Baller Within*, which he made available for the guys to check out. The first player to check out the book was RJ.

RJ, who read the book in a week, was a team leader and was fed up with the losing culture he had endured for three years, including an embarrassing 19-game losing streak. He was hungry for solutions with his team's inept play on the field. He knew that a mindset shift had to happen for this transformation to occur. What was most interesting was that RJ was the smallest player on the roster, 5-foot-6, 145 pounds. How was this guy going to inspire his team to win? By simply adopting the principles in the book: goal setting and working with a relentless pursuit.

RJ built confidence in the locker room, speaking to his team about brotherhood, belief and giving maximum effort. Before the season, I came to the school to give a motivational talk to the team. After hearing about RJ, I wanted to meet him. During the talk, I fed off of RJ's push for motivation and team camaraderie, ensuring that all team members are each responsible for their success. RJ was convinced in this ideology and was confident his team would show this in their first game. He led the charge throughout the season.

In the end, the team was successful, finishing with a three-seven record. This was all built on the leadership of RJ. Here are the stages of RJ's transformation which changed culture of his team well after he graduated.

RJ identified the problem (team morale low, dismal record)

RJ sought out counsel from coach (inquired about solutions, best practices)

Coach honored his request (acquired positive resources to address the issues)

RJ accepted his leadership role (reading the book, gaining needed insights)

Coach provided additional resources (hired speaker to reinforce RJ's newfound principles)

RJ inspired others to join him in leadership (with the help of coaches, captains are selected)

The rest is history. After the 2012 (three-seven) season, the team went on to have three consecutive years of winning seasons, two years making the playoffs and the third year winning a playoff game. RJ, the small in stature, big in heart football player, created a movement.

The moral of the story: a mindset shift, seeking out resources and a relentless pursuit for winning in life is possible. When you decide to keep showing up for your life goals, you create opportunities that you didn't even know existed.

48 HOUR RULE

If you are like me, you've probably had the experience of finding a really great idea that you jot down. Then, you go on to your usual activities, and that great idea that you know without doubt would make a difference fades away. In this era with an information overload the next good book, video, or podcast competes for your attention. It's true that you will not benefit from any of it if you don't use it. One technique to overcome this is to put that good idea to work within 48 hours.

Whether these good ideas come from a conference speaker, a book, a podcast, or video, capture the essence of it, then write down three key things that you can use at once. Incorporate these into your plans for the next day or week. This allows you to immediately test the idea and make adjustments.

This practice helps you be highly motivated and invested as you continue seeking and absorbing valuable information. The 48-hour rule helps you put to work that great idea instead of being buried in your stacks of notebooks, self-help books and other programs that you intend to implement.

The 48-Hour rule is an effective way to use what you've learned within days and making it part of your success strategy.

KEEP A TIGHT CIRCLE

Recognize that everyone grows at a different pace. This is important as you press forward with your goals and plans.

One change that is difficult is your circle of friends who may no longer fit like they once did. Truth is, some of them you will outgrow. Take an honest look at the people you spend the most time with. It's not by accident that all of you have something in common. Whether it is your place of work, the gym, church or hobbies and recreation, similar interest are present. Then, as your mindset shifts in support of your new goals, the people you spent time with may seem different. In fact, it is you who has changed, not your friends.

There's no reason to be judgment or critical.

When I started my first company in my early 20s, my father told me, "Son, as you continue to progress in life and continue to build on your success and continue earning, you will lose friends as you elevate."

I didn't want to believe this until I saw it unfold over the next decade. When this occurs, allow it to simply be. No need for arguments of confrontations, just let it go naturally. Honor the values and commitments you have and move on.

One more thing about those friends. At some point, as their mindset evolves and they also change, and they may become friends again. Some may move in and out of your life, and some may be gone for good. Either way, accept these relationships for the gifts they are, for however long they last.

Final Thoughts on Seeking Counsel with Dr. Greg Reid

Actively Seek Guidance

How important has seeking guidance been to your overall success?

Seeking guidance has been paramount for my success in life and has given me the opportunity to impact the lives of others. I have a philosophy that you seek counsel, not opinion. Counsel is based on wisdom, knowledge, and mentorship, whereas opinion is based on ignorance, lack of knowledge and inexperience. If you go to a family friend and say you are starting a new venture, they might try to protect you and talk you out of it, especially if they have never done it themselves. But if you go to a world authority, a credible source who's already accomplished what you want and ask for guidance, they will give you counsel based on wisdom, knowledge, and mentorship. They can actually give you the blueprint for success.

Name a time in your life or professional career when you felt seeking guidance was most effective.

When I wanted to become a bestselling author, I went to Barnes and Nobles. I did not go to the best written books. I did not want to be a great-writing author. I wanted to be a best-selling author, so I went to the bestsellers section. I asked those authors how they accomplished it. Then, I added my own spin, my own system, and here we are today with over 100 projects in circulation and twenty-eight bestsellers. I've also done this in my personal life when I climbed Mount Kilimanjaro. I hired the top people who have climbed it a total of 900 times. Where they put their blueprint, I put my blueprint. Even when I decided to run with the bulls, I found the person who wrote the definitive book on running with the bulls. I asked them where I needed to stand to have the greatest and safest experience. I had the achievement of doing something that most can only dream of. And you can do the same.

How would you advise someone who has been reluctant to ask for guidance in pursuing their goals?

You are where you choose to be. So, if you choose to stay where you are, then you cannot blame other people for your setbacks and circumstances. On the same note, the most successful people are also the most available people. I suggest you create a hit list and spend thirty minutes a day reaching out to people. Surround yourself with people you have respect for, not people you have influence over. If you say you want to connect with astronauts, make a hit list of the living astronauts and everyday reach out (via direct message) to them on Instagram, Facebook, Twitter, and other social media platforms. In the message say, "listen, I'd like 12.5 minutes of your time, I want to ask you one simple question about your time in space and I promise I will end the conversation after the 12.5 minutes. It would be an honor to speak with you." That specificity will open many doors of opportunity for you and provide much-needed counsel.

In addition to seeking guidance, what is another important
principle that you use that has been beneficial to your success?
I like to refer to CPC: Clues, Patterns and Choices. It works like this: take accountability and responsibility for things that happen to you and stop blaming other people. For example, if you go out on a first date and the woman is 20 minutes late, you see a little red flag. That's a clue. But if you go on the fifth, sixth or seventh date and she's 20 minutes late each time, that forms the "P" for pattern. Now it's your "C" choice whether you continue to deal with it, yell at her or break up with her. At this point, it's not her fault. She's just late. Stop trying to change people to fit into your paradigm. It's the same thing as seeing a rattlesnake rattle bite your kid sister. Then you go to pet the snake and get bit also. Do

you get mad at the snake? Have accountability and responsibility and know that you can change your life.

Please share some parting words for those who need an added push and words of encouragement to begin pursuing their life goals with a sense of purpose.

Get a buddy system. Because sometime what you need to do is to surround yourself with people who believe in you and can see the potential that you cannot see in yourself at times. It's so important to form either a mastermind group, or to join one, to help separate you from the ninety-five percent who just dream of success, to the top five percent who actually achieve it.

Bio: For over twenty-five years, Greg Reid has inspired millions of people to take personal responsibility to step into the potential of their greatness and, as such, his life of contribution has been recognized by government leaders, a foreign Princess as well as luminaries in education, business, and industry. Mr. Reid has been published in over 100 books including thirty-two best-sellers in forty-five languages.

Titles such as *Stickability: The Power of Perseverance; The Millionaire Mentor and Three Feet from Gold: Turn Your Obstacles into Opportunities*, have inspired countless readers to understand that the most valuable lessons we learn, are also the easiest ones to apply. Dr. Reid is known best for being Founder of Secret Knock, a *Forbes* and *Inc. Magazine* top-rated event focused on partnership, networking, and business development.

BONUS—Chapter 6:

Give

Def: to put something into the possession of someone, or to offer something for consideration as appropriate, especially to a higher authority

"Live the best life you can then give it all away."
– Melvin Moore

AFFIRMATION: I have all that I need at this moment, with more than enough to share with others.

Give. Give again. Give More. Repeat.

This chapter is the finale, a bonus, and the perfect bow on top to help you create your best life. My hope is that you implement the principles within this book to achieve all you set out to do. While this is the final chapter, it is one of the most important. Seriously, this is the cornerstone of life: giving.

Service and giving are energy that show appreciation for the blessings you have received in your life. In fact, the good you currently have is a result of you giving. You may be asking, "How?" In simple terms, you gave your talents, skills, determination, and time to achieve your goals. Along the way, you probably shared your skills and talents with people who helped you along the way. You received something for that giving, including income, satisfaction, relationships, education, and so on. Giving and receiving are always a circle, and one is incomplete without the other. So, it stands to reason, when you give more, you receive more. You can probably name instances of this in your own life.

Giving is an act of love that may be grounded in your own moral barometer or in your religion. Your giving might be your time or your money to a person, group, an organization, or a community. Giving is also an act of gratitude that mostly does not require permission, done without prior knowledge or anonymously.

PASS IT ON

You have probably had the experience of receiving an unexpected gift, and you've probably also been in a position to give an unexpected gift to someone else. Both feel good, right?

One illustration of this in my own experience was years ago when I had the opportunity to present an inspirational message to youth and teen ministries. I chose to tithe my services as a labor of love as a way of thanking the man who set this up. He had been supporting me for years. I had no expectations other than to serve a group I had committed my life to: our youth, who are the future.

The first talk, in Pearland, Texas, was with a group of teens, who warmly received me and took in my message filled with ideas to improve their lives. At the conclusion, the leader presented me with a plaque and card in appreciation, an unexpected act of kindness. I was grateful and thanked him for allowing me to share with his teens, especially because I was in the midst of a personal crisis. At the time, I was living with a fraternity brother after I was displaced from my home during my divorce. When I arrived home that night, I opened the card with its message of appreciation and a totally unexpected twenty-five dollar gift card. I could have used that money, but as I shared the news and experience with my fraternity brother, I knew the better thing was to give him the gift card, my way of letting him know that I appreciated his generosity and hospitality. I would not have been able to share a message with the teens had it not been for his charity in allowing me into his home. Of course, he was also grateful and shocked. But that wasn't the end of the story.

He, too, is a man of great faith and a giving heart who passed my gift along to the daughter of his next-door neighbor who had just graduated from high school. She and her father were, of course, thankful and thrilled. It felt like and was perfect symmetry of God in action the passing on of this gift that compounded gratitude. How beautiful that one act of love rippled forward again and again.

Be mindful of the choices you make and those you serve. All it takes is one yes and many lives can be changed for the better. Imagine how you can give your own labors of love and become a blessing to those in need. A Chinese proverb advises, "What you send out, comes back. What you sow, you reap. What you give, you get. What you see in others exists in you. Remember, life is reflective. It always gets back to you. So, give goodness." There are many in need and if you are able and willing, act now.

SEEK WAYS TO SERVE

"The meaning of life is to find your gift. The purpose of life is to give it away." These are the words of artist Pablo Picasso. This book, "*Now What,*" is structured to help you find your gifts and to meet your goals. This chapter is a recognition that meaningful lives are those in service to a cause greater than a single individual. Think about the people in your own life that you admire most. What qualities do those people embody? I bet most of them serve their larger community in some way that made them beloved. No matter how little they may have, they find a way to be of service.

If you were to make a pledge to give more of yourself, what might that be like?

My passion is helping young people, and the summer of 2017, a football camp caught my interest. It was an all-encompassing experience where the athletes were taught table etiquette, resume-building, entrepreneurship and even yoga. The camp had an outreach program to support underprivileged athletes that was supported by donations. I wanted to work with this camp hosted by Northeast Texas Community College (NTCC), and so I applied, repeatedly to pursue this opportunity. I soon learned that donations supporting the camp were too small that year to hire a speaker like me. So, the proposal I made was to donate my time to the event. This was the beginning of my commitment to a service project while in the area where I am working. Both my opportunities to be paid for speaking and my opportunities to give back to communities have grown since then. I was able to prove to myself that when my intentions are focused on providing value and giving more of myself, great things can happen.

A postscript to my story illustrates this. In this same community, I was determined to find another service project after the camp ended, an endeavor the NTCC administrator agreed to help with. When he gave me the news that he could not find any service project opportunities for me during the weekend I was in town, I was baffled and deeply disappointed because there was clearly a need. The solution he offered nearly brought me to tears.

While there were no service opportunities at that moment, he told me about a leadership conference NTCC was hosting that fall and asked me to speak.

How in the world did this happen? At this time, my entire mindset was focused on giving back to the student-athletes and kids at a football camp, all during a period when I was struggling financially. The desire to be of service returned to me blessings that were already in motion without my knowing. This way of doing business, which began during a low point in my life, became a new blueprint for my professional and business philosophy. Give first. That is worth repeating. Give first. Then give more to set the conditions for future prosperity. NTCC became a solid client.

FAITH WORKS

If one of you says to them, "Go in peace; keep warm and well fed," but does nothing about their physical needs, what good is it? In the same way, faith by itself, if it is not accompanied by action, is dead.

These words from the book of James explain the essence of faith in action. This example has two underlying meanings. It is not enough to simply say that you want someone to be well, do better and get a job, along with a plethora of other issues they may be dealing with. If you are able to give, do so. Giving may be in the form of providing advice, making a call to position someone for a job, setting up an individual with an opportunity, mentoring them, or making a financial contribution to help them get started. This statement can be said many times over: there is no shortage of good will that you can provide in the world.

COMMUNITY BUILDING

Albert Schweitzer said, "Even if it's a little thing, do something for those who have need of a man's help– something for which you get no pay but the privilege of doing it. For, remember, you don't live in a world all your own. Your brothers are here, too."

An important aspect of society has gotten lost, the importance of community. While it is important to build and create for your family and yourself, contributions to your community cannot be overlooked. Community building is a grassroots effort that focuses on the local level.

Make plans each month to committing two hours a month to a non-profit organization. Shelters and churches are seeking volunteers like you for service projects. Go to your local library and read to kids, help pass out food to the homeless or volunteer at your school district.

Choose your cause to support and act in accordance with its purpose and mission. Perhaps it's teen pregnancy, mental health, mentorship, or childhood hunger. One program that is doing great work in the Houston area (and likely in other areas also) is the Buddy Backpack Program, which provides weekend meals for at-risk children who have little to no access to nutritious meals away from school. Your participation in whatever program you choose may be with your time or with our financial support, and administrators of these programs almost always say that no gift is too small. Theodore Roosevelt said, "Do what you can, with what you have, right where you are."

Your brothers and sisters need you, and you likely know who they are. Show up, give, and serve. All that is required is your willingness.

GRATITUDE NOTES

Whether you are in the process of working toward a new goal or have already achieved prior ones, embrace gratitude, especially for the people who have helped you along the way. Be grateful and express it. A text or email periodically is nice, but those lack significance of a handwritten note.

Try this: Pick up a few packs of thank you cards, which usually come in packs of ten, twenty, or fifty that reflect your likes and personality. Send thank you cards, at least twice a year, to all who have contributed to your success. Make your notes personal and specific, something that the two of you remember and can relate to. Getting a card in the mail will touch the people receiving it and will make them feel special and appreciated.

Adding a gift card or gift certificate could be a nice gesture to those you want to give an extra thanks to. One of my favorites are Starbucks five dollar gift cards that I purchase four at a time. This is an inexpensive and kind gesture to those who have worked with you. If you know the recipient's interests, give a gift certificate for a store they frequent. This expresses gratitude in action. Commit to this. Others like to feel appreciated, just as you do. Be the example, set the tone and watch the blessings flow back to you. With good blessings, good fortunes are destined to manifest.

GET USED

There is no need to ponder on if God wants to use you in a special. You only need to seek what it is that He wants you to do. Will you stand for this truth, allowing this vision to be your own abide to His calling, as Rickie Byars beautifully sang in *Use Me*. The message of the song is an invitation to remember the meaning and impact of your choices go well beyond your life. Remember, your service to others is a ministry whether you subscribe to a particular faith system or not. Your work and life matters. In the larger sense, your life's work has benefits that extend further than your start and finish. Your presence creates for others even if you are not readily made aware of it.

The suggestion of being used for a greater good goes beyond your immediate family, who obviously benefits from your contributions. This awareness is a mindset that allows you to extend yourself in ways that you may not have otherwise planned for.

When I was in my late twenties, a long-time member of my childhood church congregation passed away. Though I had known her only through my childhood in Sunday school, I knew how beloved she was for her kindness and generosity. My dad asked me to speak at her funeral, a great honor since she was so beloved. The final words of my talk were these.

"Ask not how many people will mourn you when you die, but how many were better off because you lived."

To this day, I do not know whom to attribute this quote to, but I've never forgotten these words. It is the true essence of life. This is a life worth living and pursuing.

In your daily encounters, be a vessel, a blessing, a gift. You just need to be ready and willing to answer the call and allow yourself to be used.

HARVEY GENEROSITY

Have you paid attention to the stories of the neighbor-helping neighbors during and after natural disasters? This is giving at its finest, which I got to witness and be part of during Hurricane Harvey in 2017. This Category 4 storm dumped fifty inches of rain in four days on Houston, Texas and its surrounding counties. Beneath the record billions of dollars of damages are thousands of personal stories of homes lost and lives forever changed.

During my adult life, I have felt this sad and painful twice before: the 9/11 attacks and the Shuttle Columbia disaster.

While this was a grim and horrific time in the history of Houston and the state of Texas, there was some beauty that emerged from this. A real sense of humanity, gratitude, love, and unity filled the hearts and streets.

I was staying with my brother during the storm, which did not flood. As we checked on friends and extended families, many were being flooded out of their homes. We were like others in our fortunate situation, taking them in as they fled from their flooded homes without a second thought. Everyone pitched in to make room for two additional families. The groceries found to feed everyone felt a bit like the loaves and fishes that multiplied to feed the masses during Jesus' Sermon on the Mount. Our time together with these thirteen people in my brother's home was filled with fellowship and surprising good cheer while we rode out this historic catastrophe.

Even before the storm ended, people mobilized to help. Those with boats organized on Facebook and went into flooded neighborhoods to assist the National Guard and local officials evacuate trapped families and their pets by the hundreds. After the water receded, youth groups, community groups, and church members organized to help homeowners get their ruined belongings out of houses and stripped the drywall down to the studs so things could begin to dry. Everyone who could help in some way did in acts large and small, from providing water and sandwiches to the volunteers to taking in mountains of laundry and returning it clean and dry.

All of this was so inspiring that I was even more eager to serve my community. I had the privilege of working with my sister at the community college in Cypress collecting and organizing donations for two days. What was astounding was the generosity. The location was soon filled to capacity with clothes of every size for children and adults, diapers, sheets, and towels. When we had taken in all that we could, we directed people to a nearby church also collecting donations. Within hours, they had also reached capacity. The work was difficult, and the hours were long, and every single one of us was blessed by the energy of giving. It was a labor of love.

One night a segment on the local news showed the depth and breadth of the good trying to manifest during this catastrophe by showing a line with thousands of people waiting. What were they waiting for? Not for food, shelter, or benefits. It was thousands showing up each day, from all over the city, to volunteer their time and service. It was living proof that the human spirit is eager to give, love, and care for one another. This experience is easily the most memorable of my life, and I am blessed beyond anything I could have imagined to have been a part of it.

Here's the truth: you don't need anyone's permission to extend a helping hand. No one will stop you. Just do it. You never know, your gesture may be the one that changes the life of someone forever.

MAMA SHOWED ME

My mother gave me two especially valuable pieces of advice during those years I was growing up and rode to school with her every morning: love is all that matters and that I should be unafraid to go after what I wanted. She might have been whispering in Lenny Kravitz's ear when he wrote the hit *Always on the Run* because I hear her voice first when he sings about what mama said and the good advice she had.

She was an example of someone who gave her life to her calling. Teaching, which she did for well over forty years, was and always will be her purpose and love of life. To this day, I still run into people who credit their success to my mother. She was a powerhouse in the classrooms, but it was her works behind the scenes that are the most remembered.

During my elementary school years, I naturally rode to school with her, and like all teachers, her days were long, and I often waited while she was on duty for bus and car riders and of course, after school suspension. She also had great relationships with the cafeteria works and the janitors, which seemed ordinary to me at the time.

After I was in college and came to visit my mother at the school, I noticed how every janitor was elated when she passed by. She always introduced them to me along with some personal bit of information about them. I realized these warm interactions were not quite the same as other teachers. What was it about my mother that the custodians, and also cafeteria workers, not just happy, but besides themselves when mom was around? I asked her why the cafeteria workers and janitors love you so much?"

Her answer was on point and revealed a valuable lesson. She said to me,

"Son, these men and women work hard and rarely do they get respect from anyone. Sometimes people overlook them, and some talk down to them. They are important part of the school running each day. They come in early and stay late. Most of them don't make much money, but they are good people and I want to make sure they know someone cares."

When I learned that she often bought them a breakfast or lunch, I realized I had learned that lesson from her since it was a practice I had adopted. She recognized the good people who looked out for her and did her best to take care of them. I've done my best to embody her advice of, "Ahmard, always look out for the people who cook, clean and do some of the dirty work wherever you do business. They deserve respect and can make your job better when you acknowledge them as important."

That moment was integral life lesson learned, to be respectful of everyone regardless of class or status. The same principle is valuable for you today.

Perhaps it is the employee at your favorite coffee shop who provides you a smile daily, the postal worker who delivers your mail with a pleasant attitude, or the security guard who is there before you get to the office and is there long after you leave. All of these people are part of your life. Take the time to recognize them. They are important, and they deserve your respect. Maybe buy them lunch, give them a written thank you card or buy them a donut and coffee on your way in to work. All of these acts of giving and love will indeed make their day. Remember two things: each of us needs all of us, and for any of these actions you choose to make, there is no permission needed.

DO UNTO OTHERS

Do unto others as you would have them do unto you.

These are the words of Jesus from the Sermon on the Mount, the "Golden Rule." Simple words, right? Like many simple things, the practice is not easy. You cannot wait for someone else to go first. It must begin with you. Give to others and increase will be given back to you. Whatever you want must be given first. Love will be reciprocated. When you serve, you will change lives, and you will be changed in the process. All of these things you do from the heart will return multiplied many times over. Do not be concerned about the how, when or from whom. Rewards will come to you in unexpected ways. This is a spiritual principle that has an undefeated return rate.

Focus on your giving, your work, and its impact. That is your primary role in the transaction. Allow God and spiritual laws of life to handle the rest.

FINAL THOUGHTS

No matter the profession you pursue or business you create, you always want to embody the mindset of giving more than you are earning. Service and giving creates their own energy that makes you a magnet for expanding good in and for the world around you. What's beautiful is giving always produces a return of compensation mentally, spiritually, and financially. It bears repeating, "how many people were better off because you lived?" Live by that truth and you will be blessed well beyond your years on earth.

Final Thoughts on Giving with Larisa Miller

Giving is Essential for Success in Life and Business

How important has giving back been to your overall success?
Giving has been one of my key pillars. Your business is only as successful as the community that it serves, not the com-

munity that serves the business. So, it's essential that all businesses recognize that they must have a conscience, as they are an integral part of society. Giving back is so important to generating value for the stakeholders and the customers.

Name a time in your life or professional career where giving back was most effective in changing lives.

It's been one of the fundamental pillars of my life. When I was an army wife, and I couldn't work because we moved every two years, I was one of the highest volunteer hour military spouses in the army. So, it's always been fundamental for me. There is something about the culture of giving back. For me, it's my drug of choice because there's a feeling you get when you give to someone who can never repay you. The feeling of making someone smile when they have few reasons to smile is a feeling you can't measure. It's about quiet giving, genuine giving, and genuine service. That's the foundation of a successful business, to give back. When you give back you receive many times over. All businesses must have a conscience and have a policy of corporate social responsibility. Businesses must make sure to create an environment of giving a habit, even amongst employees. You need to recognize that they have a responsibility to support their local community.

Is there a specific project or accomplishment in which giving to a person, group or cause was most imperative to you?

For me, that would probably have to be my time in refugee camps. It's not one specific event, but every time I would interact with the refugee camps. Working on behalf of a nonprofit, you see people whose lives have been completely turned upside down through circumstances that they did nothing to create. They were forced to leave their homes and start over. Many are highly educated engineers, scientists, and doctors and now they are peddling oranges and water to be able to feed their families. Yet they would offer me a simple act of kindness by welcoming me into their tents in the refugee camps. They offered me food, which is all the food they have to feed their entire family for a night. Their hospitable giving was so strong, those simple acts of kindness, in sharing with strangers. I stopped to think how many times we would do that in reverse here in our country (America). If someone came to our door, would we welcome them in and them in and give them all the food we had for our entire family as act of hospitality and kindness? I think generally the answer is no. Here you have people who have almost nothing, and yet, even with nothing, they are willing to share with a stranger out of simple gratitude for their kindness and giving. Every time I've interacted in the refugee camps, I've come away a different person, a better person.

How would you advise someone who has not seen giving back as an important aspect of life?

Giving back needs to be a part of your fundamental culture. It needs to be written into every single business plan, business strategy and major goal from the very first moment the plan comes into being. I work with entrepreneurs around the country as they are looking at starting their own new businesses and I tell them right from the beginning, you have a responsibility to give back. As you write your business plan, automatically allocate a certain percentage that you will pledge for your social responsibility and give back. If you do that, giving becomes a habit and part of your business culture. You are changing lives and making an impact without the business feeling it. For you, individually, you want to feel it, as the act of giving is important and significant. That's why it's essential. Companies that give back don't just choose mindless acts of social responsibility by writing a one-off check. It's important to find something that resonates with you, develop your own company projects around that and encourage your employees to give as well. Your employees can use their time as volunteers or have a small amount automatically deducted out of their paychecks. It's essential for all businesses of the future to not only have a conscience, but to make sure the entire business ecosystem is representative of a culture that gives back.

In addition to giving back for the greater good, what is another important principle that has been beneficial to your success?
Empathy. I've had the honor and privilege of being able to have experiences most Americans, specifically an American female, doesn't typically get to have. I've visited rural villages in Africa, Yemen, Jordan, and Iraq, seeing the value in people and learning great lessons from them. I found that there's some great innovations and ideas that are trapped in

the minds of people around the world. These people may never be discovered because they don't have the opportunity to do so. They have limited access to education to give them the ability to envision what they can do with their ideas. For me, it's having empathy and understanding that people are people around the world, despite their ethnicity, gender, race, or socioeconomic status, all have something to contribute. At the end of the day, we are all similar. When you look at the youth in rural Africa or those in a refugee camp, you can't help but think that the next great invention, technological innovation, or cure for a disease could be trapped inside the mind of one of those youths. They may never get the opportunity to bless the world with that idea. So, it behooves us as global citizens to make sure to prioritize a global perspective to give back. There's a need to recognize that people are people, and they need all of us to have a sense of social responsibility and commitment.

Please share some parting words for those who need an added push and words of encouragement to begin pursuing their life goals with a sense of purpose.

The easy answer is people just quit too easily. And while that is true, I find that to be the biggest impediment to people who have a hard time achieving their goals.

People set the largest goal they can for themselves, and the minute they have a setback or two, they see that goal as so far away and unattainable that they give up. And while it's important to set the largest goal you can have for yourself;

you have to set small achievable benchmarks and milestones along the way so that you can have small successes. You want to see yourself progressing and moving forward. Along with the ability to make a decision, it's enough to keep you on the track to your goals and achieving your dreams. Too often people can't make a decision, or they'll ask six, ten or fifteen people their opinion before making a decision. I'm one who firmly believes that if you have a decision to make, make that decision, believe in that decision, and see it through to the end. Sometimes the end is bitter and sometimes it's sweet, but either way you'll learn the greatest life lessons.

Bio: Larisa Miller is CEO of Phoenix Global, a global boutique consulting firm, and subsidiary, Phoenix Global Purveyors, serves as distributors of fine food and beverage products from international markets. Larisa has recently been named one of the World's Top 100 People in Finance by *Top 100 Magazine*; one of the 10 Most Influential Business Leaders of 2020 by *Exeleon Magazine*; 100 Global Women of Excellence by *Sovereign Magazine*, Top 10 Most Influential Friends of Africa by *For Business in Africa Magazine*, and the 2020 Personality of the Year by *Powerhouse Magazine*.

Larisa studied Political Science with a minor in Hungarian at Rutgers University in New Brunswick, New Jersey, and Organizational Leadership at Penn State University. She worked for the Commonwealth of Pennsylvania for the Secretary and Deputy Secretary of Agriculture, and later for the Pennsylvania Governor, Tom Ridge, with a focus on public policy. Larisa spent several years working as a personal advisor and head of business development a member of the Royal Family in Abu Dhabi, United Arab Emirates, with focus on investment in sustainable development, technology, energy, and agriculture. Additionally, Larisa served as head of the Royal Family's large non-profit foundation, Circle of Hope, which focused on women, youth, literacy, and education. Through her work with this UAE-based foundation, Larisa spent considerable time working with women and children in refugee camps in the Middle East and Africa.

Chapter 7:

Now What - Gratitude Lists

Affirmation: On this day, I promise to give more of myself, to become more of myself and encourage others to do the same. I am the Gamechanger the world is waiting to see. I accept this challenge.

To have an attitude of gratitude is a prerequisite to increase in all areas of your life: physical, mental, spiritual, financial, social, professional and familial. That's right. Be grateful before becoming the powerhouse of service you intend to become by applying the principles in this book. Gratitude helps you recognize your blessings right now. Your good exists now. It's true that you may not be where you want to be, but be thankful for your life, those who love you and the accomplishments you've achieved.

As you complete this book, start a gratitude list. Start with building a Top Ten list of things you are grateful for. Once you get the flow of this, you may want to add two to three items more to the list every day. It does not matter how big or small or how important or insignificant the items on your list are. The important part is creating the habit and cultivating the mindset that you have many positives all around you. Keep your list close and repeat it to yourself when you awaken. Reading and repeating all that you are grateful for will keep you in a positive frame of mind as you create more of the positive energy you seek. Here are a few from my personal list that I started some time ago.

- I am grateful for God, the all-powerful, all-knowing loving spirit who blesses me with life.
- I am I am grateful for a father and mother who raised me in a loving fashion.
- I am grateful that my parents emphasized the importance of being respectful of my fellow man.
- I am grateful that I was taught the importance of education and continued learning.
- I am grateful to possess good health and a mind to create.
- I am grateful for an immediate family who loves and supports me and my efforts.

- I am grateful to live in a free country that has given me the opportunity to produce wealth for myself and others.
- I am grateful that I have created programs and services to help empower people.
- I am grateful for every friend, colleague, coworker, and client who has supported mentally, financially, and spiritually.
- I am grateful for my next breath which my Father in Heaven has blessed me with.

Now implement a spirit of gratefulness. You will feel the power of your mind when you take the time to acknowledge how grateful and blessed you are. Invest time into creating and adding to your gratitude list. The more you are grateful for what is in your life today, the more you will have to be grateful for in your life tomorrow. Trust that you will not be disappointed, and trust, that you will feel empowered.

Chapter 8:

Now What - Go-Getters Prayer

Dear Heavenly Father,

First, I thank you for this very moment I am spending with you. Thank you for the next breath of life.

As I prepare for the busy day ahead, give me the wisdom to be able to maintain my composure.

Help me to remain steadfast on the day ahead.

I pray that my mind remained focused on creation.

You promised me that what I ask for in faith is destined to happen. As your beloved child, I believe in your power and strength. I thank you for the talents and abilities you've blessed me with so I can make useful contributions to the world.

For any task that tests me mentally and physically, give me the courage to press forward no matter the circumstances before me.

Take care of me in this moment and during the day as I work towards a favorable outcome for my family at home, my team, my company, and my colleagues.

Acknowledging the Spirit within me and a positive, winning mindset, I affirm that success is being created now, and is ongoing throughout the day.

You said that where I am, you are there also. In this time of my expanded awareness, I am in need of your counsel and wisdom. I trust that my request is being fulfilled. This is my bold prayer.

I pray for a receptive mind and an open heart. It is said that because of you my existence is chosen for this time in history. For this divine right timing I say Thank You Father, Thank You.

As this day comes to a close, I honor you first before celebrating all that was accomplished on this day.

In this present moment, my life is in service to you, and I acknowledge my fulfilled desires come through you. I can be assured my requests are already done.

Thank You and Amen.

Thank You/Call to Action

Whether you purchased this book, received as a gift, or borrowed it off the shelf of a friend, thank you for supporting the *Now What* message and movement. It is our hope and intention that you found value within these pages and have begun making meaningful changes in your life as of right now.

For additional resources, please visit Ahmard's website at ahmardvital.com, where you can find videos and resources. You may also fill out the contact form located there if you seek individual mental performance coaching.

To book Ahmard for an empowering, inspirational, and motivational keynote for your team, company, or organization, click the "Book Ahmard" tab on the website. For program details and to fill out our Pre-Event Questionnaire, visit: www.ahmardvital.com/booknow or call our office at 832-577-1911.

Bookings/Media Appearance:

Soul Player Media – jcooks@soulplayermedia.com

Follow us on all social media platforms @ahmardvital on Instagram and Facebook.

About the Author

Ahmard Vital

Motivational consultant, international speaker, and author Ahmard Vital has empowered people globally with his inspirational guidance and tips for self-development. Ahmard provides his audiences with the tools needed to achieve personal success, utilize willpower and determination, and develop strategies that will allow people of all ages to achieve personal and professional excellence.

After nearly a decade of studying the performance habits of high achieving athletes, Ahmard has developed programs of inspiration and motivation that are beneficial to individuals, professionals, companies, and organizations worldwide.

In 2011, Ahmard published *Awaken the Baller Within*, which was quickly labeled as the "athlete's life manual" by some pundits in sports media. This book was taught in more than a dozen colleges and close to fifty athletic departments and sports camps. As a mental performance coach, Ahmard helped secure more than $6 million dollars in scholarship monies and worked with athletes at the Division I level and the National Football League.

Not long after a successful career as a college football recruiting analyst with Scout.com, a Fox Sports affiliate, Ahmard founded That Guy Media Group and expanded his platform to small business and nonprofit organizations where he focused on dream building, goal setting, and a relentless pursuit of the aforementioned. By teaching his audiences to recognize their strengths, and capitalize on the power that everyone harnesses within, individuals can realize previously unimagined levels of personal happiness and success

Ahmard is becoming one of the most sought-after motivational speakers in the world, working in countries like Zambia and Abu Dhabi (UAE). In the United States, he's inspired professionals at companies like the Boys and Girls Club, MD Anderson Cancer Center, and the Salvation Army. His college clients include Prairie View A&M, Houston Community College and West Texas A&M.

He published his second book, *I Am More Than Enough*, in April 2019 to address many of his clients' confidence challenges in their personal and professional lives. When Ahmard is not traveling, speaking, or writing, he works as a humanitarian and teen ministry leader, volunteering his time to inspire youth to envision their futures beyond their challenges and circumstances. He is also an avid reader and fitness coach, teaching cycling classes in North Houston.

Glossary

3G APPROACH. A first-thing-in-the-morning practice to set the tone for your day by writing two statements of gratitude (I am grateful for _____) and a goal statement that identifies one achievable goal for the day.

3x10 Technique. A strategy to learn more effectively by practicing a skill three times with a ten-minute rest period in between each session

10X Rule. A process to create a dominant mindset that thinks bigger and is willing to give more to achieve goals. "Imagine ten times more." A dream ten times bigger may be more inspiring than the smaller one you first envisioned. Imagine giving your goal ten times more than what you believe it will take to achieve it.

48 Hour Rule. A strategy of applying new ideas or skills within forty-eight hours to ensure you get the most out of them.

AA. An acronym for Accountability Ally. This is a trusted person you regularly check in with who holds you accountable to do what you have agreed you will do to achieve your goals.

Big 5 of Planning. Consists of five items. *Identify* the goal. *Justify* why you want it. *Specify* what you want with clarity and precision. *Quantify* your goal by the time, effort, and material its achievement requires. *Magnify* your desire and enthusiasm by imagining your goal in as full and robust way as possible.

G.O.D. An acronym for Good on Demand. No matter what you call the intuitive force within you, its guidance is always working to supply the Good you seek. This energy force is always present within you and is always working to manifest your Good, as revealed by Jesus when he said, "Whatever you ask for in faith shall be given to you."

I AM. An acronym for It's All Mental. These two words are among the most powerful because they are in recognition of the self-sufficiency and self-sustaining nature of God that is present within each person who says "I am _____). This phrase should be spoken only for what you want (such as, I am powerful. I am prosperous. I am kind. I am the architect of my own life.)

Mastermind Group. A group of people who regularly meet to encourage one another toward the achievement of their (usually) separate and unrelated goals. The term mastermind was first coined by Napoleon Hill in *Think and Grow Rich* where like-minded people working in harmony with one another create a powerful, unseen positive force—a mastermind.

Pareto principle (80/20 rule). A theory that maintains eighty percent of the output or outcomes is determined by twenty percent of the input or possible factors. For example, eighty percent of the points scored are by twenty percent of the players or eighty percent of the fouls are committed by twenty percent of the players.

Parkinson's Law. A principle that says work will expand to fill the allotted time set aside to achieve a task. This is a caution to plan well and allot slightly less time to complete a task rather than slightly (or a lot) more.

See big, set small. The process of dividing lofty goals into manageable pieces. The thousand-mile journey begins with the first step, the book begins with the first word, the savings account begins with the first dollar.

Two Goals To Go. A practice of setting two, small, easy-to-achieve goals every day that contribute to the larger endeavor. This helps to keep you encouraged because you begin to see the small pieces build toward the result you want.

Work in Reverse Principle. Set your intention for the end result. Because you know where you are going, you can more easily determine the importance of interim goals and their respective tasks. This principle helps you to create manageable, effective steps to achieve the results you want for your goals.

A free ebook edition is available with the purchase of this book.

To claim your free ebook edition:

1. Visit MorganJamesBOGO.com
2. Sign your name CLEARLY in the space
3. Complete the form and submit a photo of the entire copyright page
4. You or your friend can download the ebook to your preferred device

A **FREE** ebook edition is available for you or a friend with the purchase of this print book.

CLEARLY SIGN YOUR NAME ABOVE

Instructions to claim your free ebook edition:
1. Visit MorganJamesBOGO.com
2. Sign your name CLEARLY in the space above
3. Complete the form and submit a photo of this entire page
4. You or your friend can download the ebook to your preferred device

Print & Digital Together Forever.

Snap a photo

Free ebook

Read anywhere